To Aira

Самой ... в мире.

from

Bill

The Story of the Air Age

WINGED PEACE

Also by William A. Bishop

WINGED WARFARE

The Story of the Air Age

WINGED PEACE

WILLIAM A. "BILLY" BISHOP, V.C.

With an Afterword by Arthur Bishop

McGRAW-HILL RYERSON

Montreal Toronto

Winged Peace

First published in 1944 by The Macmillan Company of Canada

Published in 1990 by
McGraw-Hill Ryerson Limited
330 Progress Avenue
Toronto, Canada
M1P 2Z5

1 2 3 4 5 6 7 8 9 10 D 1 2 3 4 5 6 7 8 9 0

Canadian Cataloguing in Publication Data
Bishop, William A., date
Winged peace

ISBN 0-07-551025-1

1. Aeronautics, Military—History. 2. Aeronautics Commercial—History. 3. Aeronautics—History. I. Title.

TL553.B58 1990 629.13′09 C90-093869-2

COVER ILLUSTRATION: PETER MOSSMAN
COVER DESIGN: SHARON MATTHEWS

Printed and bound in Canada

PREFATORY NOTE

TO TWO personal friends the author is indebted for assistance beyond measure in the preparation of this work.

Long before any of its chapters were down on paper we discussed by the hour our mutual hopes and fears as our civilization takes up the tasks of the Air Age, finding ourselves in complete agreement at every stage of innumerable talks. The urging and support of these two friends had much to do with the decision to write this book, their counsel and advice even more with its preparation.

The first of these is Charles Villiers, whose reputation as an aircraft designer, an engineer, and one of the most brilliant men in aviation today, has long since been established in Britain. He is, as well, a man of clear social and political insight, who has consistently related in his mind the implications of global and stratospheric flight to the people who must live in the same world with these new developments of science. In particular I must extend my thanks to Mr. Villiers for the assistance he has rendered with that part of the book which relates to the new propulsion units and the revolution in the realm of flight which their coming portends.

Friendship with the other member of the team, the Canadian writer, Leslie Roberts, goes back to the early months of 1917 and another war. Like myself, Leslie Roberts has never been able to divorce himself from aviation. Ever since the First World War he has been writing about it, flying to all manner of strange places in all manner of strange machines during the between-wars years. When I decided to proceed to the writing of *Winged Peace,* Roberts undertook to give me assistance with the problems of research. People who have worked with him in the past have told me that Leslie Roberts is a veritable "glutton for research." If I did not believe them before, I do now. All that I can say is that without his aid, given unstintingly and often, I am sure, at sacrifice of rest, it would have been impossible for me to write *Winged Peace.*

The views and opinions expressed in this book are the personal views and opinions of the author, and must in no way be interpreted as representing those of the Canadian Government, any of the armed services, or any political party or society.

WILLIAM A. BISHOP

Contents

PART IV: ORDEAL BY AIR

PART V: WHERE DO WE GO FROM HERE?

AFTERWORD

Illustrations

THE MAPS HAVE BEEN PREPARED FOR THIS VOLUME
BY RICHARD EDES HARRISON

PHOTOGRAPHS AND MAPS FOLLOWING THE END OF THE FOREWORD, PAGE XIV

MAPS WITHIN THE TEXT

Foreword

OF ALL the strange phenomena of war none is more amazing to me than the apparent failure of the average man to recognize what has happened in the realm of aviation since Germany struck at Poland in the autumn of 1939 and mankind faced the second world war in a quarter century.

People talk of global aviation as if it were well past the corner of the next cloudbank, not as if it had become an accomplished fact. Actually aviation is the greatest single force which can ensure an enduring peace, or, on the other hand, will be the most destructive weapon man has produced in his history. That is exactly where we stand *today*. Not even all the recognized leaders in the realm of aviation appear to grasp what has happened, however. Too many of them are still thinking in terms of factors with which they dealt five years ago—comparatively slow planes of comparatively restricted range—and apparently have not noted the revolutionary changes the immediate future will bring. Primarily they seem to be worrying about the routes which are to be allotted to specific nations and people, about interests purely national in scope, about the money to be made in the world of tomorrow by carrying people, mail, and goods from one continent to another. All sort of petty bickering goes on about "chosen instruments" and free competition, about "open sky" and "closed sky." Every now and then somebody attempts a new definition of Freedom of the Air, which we have never known, and are not likely to know in the same manner in which we have known Freedom of the Seas. Gentlemen in the Senate of the United States have suggested that the various and varied facilities for flight which Uncle Sam has created in numerous parts of the world for the purpose of waging war against the Axis powers should be permanently taken over by the United States —the word "confiscated" scarcely seems too harsh—as a partial payoff for Lend-Lease. Our friends in Britain are equally concerned about what is to happen to British world-aviation interests in the days to come. In the realms of aviation and politics, then, it may be said that most of the talking is being done along lines intensely nationalistic, in so far as the two great English-speaking powers, the United States and Britain, are concerned. My own country,

Canada, I am happy to say, tends more to the co-operative approach to the problems of the future, a happy augury in the light of the favorable geographical position in which she stands, at the top of the world and the crossroads of the primary intercontinental routes. But of such matters, more later.

While all these discussions are in spate, the public, as such, remains blissfully unaware of the course of events. That is because what comes to the attention of their eyes and ears talks mainly about *tomorrow*—what tomorrow's luxury liners of the air will be like, what distant lands we shall visit some faraway tomorrow with the ease with which we visited next-door neighbors yesterday, but always tomorrow, tomorrow, tomorrow, whereas global aviation is the great phenomenon of *today*. The truth of the matter is that nations have shrunk to the size of villages and continents to the length of Main Street. The oceans of the world have become ditches. These are not things which are *going* to happen. They *have* happened.

As you are reading these paragraphs, fleets of four-engined bombers are winging non-stop from Montreal to North Africa. Others will leave North America and arrive in Karachi in less than forty hours. Men of affairs, military leaders, all manner of people engaged in important war missions are being whisked from continent to continent, not just every now and then in time of emergency, but on intercontinental shuttle routes. The globe has become a network of airways joining the United Nations. Airports in far northern Canada, adjacent to the Arctic Circle, the highway to Russia and the Orient and the main line to Tokyo, boast runways longer than any to be found on New York's crack La Guardia Field. It is possible that the Old World has been saved from the Nazi yoke by virtue of the ability of the United Nations to fly great numbers of bombers from the factories of North America to the fighting fields of Britain and Russia. Certainly it has been one of the great factors in turning the tide Freedom's way.

On the day when the shooting stops, then, our civilization will find itself fully equipped with the facilities of global flight. Our job will be to adapt those facilities to man's lawful occasions, to man's good, to man's peace. It is a task in which we shall fail again if our approach to world problems is selfishly nationalistic, or if we think only in terms of individual profits arising from commercial trai portation. Our problems go much deeper.

The first thought, then, to fix in mind, is that we can fly from anywhere to anywhere else *now*. There is no trick to it any longer. The question is: How are we going to go about regulating and controlling this great aerial juggernaut which has reduced the world to the size of a football?

All the people of the world have to be awakened to the implications of this behemoth of the skies. I am at a loss to understand how the true impact of air-power can have failed to impress them with its power and importance during the pre-invasion weeks of the spring of 1944, when every day they were reading of raids into deepest Germany in strengths of thousands of planes—America's Fortresses and Liberators by day, Britain's Lancasters and Halifaxes by night —or on June 15, 1944, when the United States government announced the performance of the B-29 in its first official combat test over Japan, and the creation of a new global air force in order best to utilize its mighty potentialities. Daily, during the pre-invasion days and later, the press and the radio drummed into our eyes and ears stories of thousands of tons of bombs which inexorably and mercilessly were reducing Nazidom's capital and many of its great industrial centers to rubble.

Perhaps constant repetition weakens the power of the story, destroys its effect upon our imagination. But surely the least airwise of us can see in these vast aerial armadas, with their clouds of fighter escorts, and in the soundly documented promises for the B-29, that the Air Age has in fact arrived, that it is no longer something in store for tomorrow. What are we going to do about it? If we think we can dispose of it simply by having a diplomats' meeting for the purpose of carving up the air routes of the world and distributing them amongst ourselves, and by developing nationally huge military air forces, we shall be much mistaken. If we approach the problem with narrow national outlook, we shall soon be taxiing out for the first take-off of World War III. In fact, I would like to go even further and use a sentence or two which I propose to discuss at length as a point of view later: *We have got to trust each other in the air. We have got to become aerial partners.* Otherwise we shall ultimately become aerial enemies again. Mankind cannot handle with too great care the new implements of warfare which his brains and hands have fashioned on the blueprint table and in the laboratory.

Here is another totally erroneous concept. Yet it is one which appears to be held even by people closely associated with aviation, some of whom still seem to think that the fundamental problem is how to affix more motors to machines and to lift greater pay-loads without having to carry too much fuel for the long hops. In other words, they fail to take note of the implications of the new and startling forms of propulsion which are just beginning to emerge, even if more or less experimentally, from the production lines.

We are standing at the threshold of stratospheric flight, of forms of human movement (and of new forms of potential destruction) which may revolutionize again all our thinking as the Age of Flight already has revolutionized it. The place to discuss these possibilities, however, is in the body of this book, not in its prefatory remarks. All that I seek to stress here is that these possibilities are here today, that they are part and parcel of the living present. That is the basic thesis of this book.

Some day soon the world will foregather at the conference table to write a new design for living. The hope of every one of us is that what will emerge will be an enduring peace, that we shall fashion a world in which man's object will be to live in accord with other men, that the policy of Good Neighborliness will become world policy, not simply a hemispheric hope. A very great part of our hope for that enduring peace will depend entirely on our approach to the new era of flight—on how well our leaders are informed concerning the implications of global aviation in the hard school of war, on how determined we are that the new implements our hands fashion shall be used to enlarge, not to constrict, man's peaceful horizons. We shall succeed only if behind our leaders is marshaled a strong and informed world opinion, an opinion sufficiently strong that these leaders will know before they assemble to write the terms of peace that the peoples of the world *demand* the Peoples' Peace they have fought to attain. That Peoples' Peace can only emerge from the Peoples' War if we realize and accept in advance the implications of what the arrival of the Air Age means.

The key to peace is in the skies. In these same skies flies the possibility of destruction more appalling than any we have known before. It is because of the urgency of this belief that I have written this book.

WILLIAM A. BISHOP

Ottawa, Canada,
June 1944.

WIDE WORLD PHOTOS

NATIONAL FILM BOARD

***THE BEGINNINGS:* On December 17, 1903, the Wright brothers made their first successful one-minute flight at Kittyhawk, N. C. Five years later they achieved a record by staying in the air over an hour. One of their machines is shown in flight (upper).**

Meanwhile Douglas McCurdy was experimenting along similar lines in Canada. On February 3, 1909, he made the British Empire's first successful heavier-than-air machine flight in his "Silver Dart" (lower) while skaters on the ice of Baddeck Bay tried to equal his air speed.

RCAF OFFICIAL PHOTO

***THE FIGHTERS*: "A little daisy of a ship" we called this best of all fighters in its day. The author and his Nieuport in 1916 (upper). But a quarter century changes men and machines (lower). The author and a Spitfire—invincible fighter of the Battle of Britain.**

PHOTO BY "FLIGHT," LONDON, COURTESY OF BRITISH INFORMATION SERVICES

PRESS ASSOCIATION, INC.

THE BOMBERS:* *The first RAF bomber, the DeHaviland DH4 (1916), carried a total load of less than 500 lbs. of 25-lb. bombs under both wings, dropping them most inaccurately from very low levels. Yet it was a whispered prophecy. Twenty-eight years later the B-29 Superfortress (shown here with its smaller parent, the B-17 Flying Fortress), with its wing-spread of 141 feet, its bomb-load measured in tons, its ocean-spanning range, and its pin-point accuracy which can select and destroy a single building from many thousand feet of altitude, fulfilled the prophecy which we of the Western Democracies had failed to heed until almost too late.

NORTH AMERICA LOOKS NORTH TO EURASIA

This orthographic projection centered near the center of the North American land mass (50 N, 95 W) proclaims the death of American isolation. Toward the southwest is the great insulating Ocean of the Pacific with only one rather long hop to the nearest of the Pacific islands. To the southeast the 1,800 mile gap can be crossed in a matter of hours by a plane, while on the northeast and northwest the steppingstones are so close that water is not an air barrier to either Europe or Asia.

EURASIA LOOKS NORTH TO NORTH AMERICA

Centered on the same meridian but across the Pole near the up-and-coming lumber port of Igarka, this map gives the World Island view of North America. The Arctic Mediterranean is shown as an arm of the North Atlantic. It is certainly an effective barrier to surface navigation except around its fringes, but as an air obstacle it has lost most of its effectiveness. That Eurasia is the ultimate in "defense in depth" is shown by the fact that the new industrial centers of Siberia are closer to North America than they are to many a strategic area of Asia.

CROSSROADS OF THE ATLANTIC

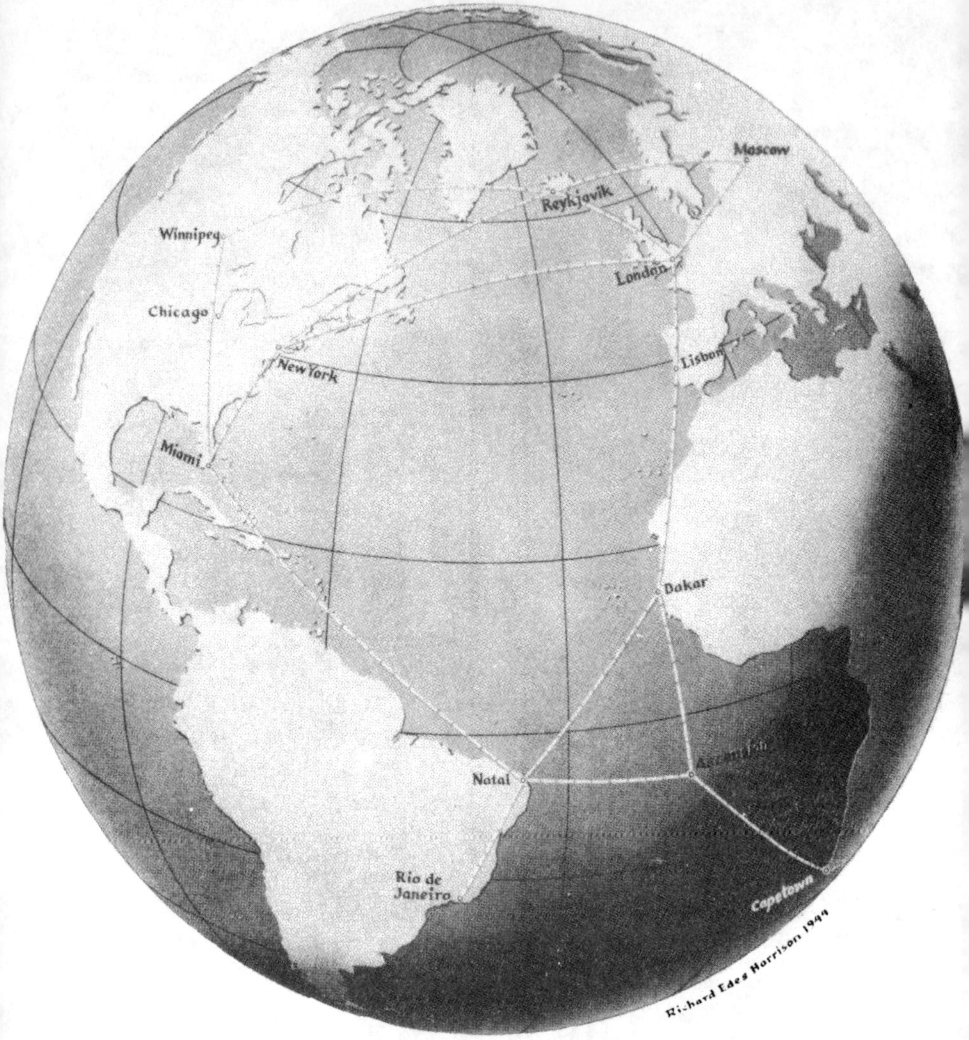

Air travel between North America and Europe, shows a strong northward trend. However until climatic obstacles are technically solved, the southern route will still be used. This map shows the propinquity of neighbors across the South Atlantic. Note how the Strait of Natal-Dakar becomes a crossroad of routes between Northern and Southern Hemispheres. [Orthographic projection centered 25 N, 40 W.]

NATIONAL FILM BOARD

PRESS ASSOCIATION, INC

***THE TRANSPORTS:* With an HS2L (upper) bought from the U.S. Government for $600, Bishop Barker Aeroplanes, Ltd., launched one of Canada's earliest commercial airlines in the face of mechanical difficulties and lack of public faith just after World War I. Twenty-five years later another good transport plane (lower), the Lockheed Constellation (8000 horse power, 62-person capacity), flew non-stop from Burbank, California, to Washington, D. C., in six hours, fifty-eight minutes.**

WIDE WORLD PHOTOS

WIDE WORLD PHOTOS

NAVAL AIRCRAFT: **On November 14, 1910, Eugene Ely foreshadowed an important element of our 1944 offensive in the Pacific by making the world's first flight from the deck of a ship (upper)—the stationary U.S.S. Birmingham. Thirty-odd years later the Grumman Avenger, audacious grandchild of the plane Ely flew, hurls itself like a rocket from a modern flat-top traveling at high speed (lower).**

PART I

The New Geography

CHAPTER 1

Curved Map vs. Flat Map

BEFORE the days of Columbus it was the average person's opinion that if you sailed west from the coast of Europe, sooner or later you would pass over the edge of the world and fall into bottomless space. Indeed, some of the scientific gentlemen of the day were convinced they were living on a flat, or wafer-like, world and everybody else took their word for it. Times have not changed as much as you think.

True, our young people today are taught in the schools that the world is globular in shape. They know that if you set off from Montreal, or New York, or San Francisco, and travel either east or west, ultimately you will return to your point of departure without turning back on your tracks. That is about all of the global conception of geography which schools teach them. Fundamentally their elders, who should be also their betters, visualize the world on which we live as they see it on a plane, with here and there colored areas and black pin-points indicating the locations of countries and cities. Our children are still being taught what may be called the geography of the flat map, a map which has no relation of any sort to the world in which they will live their lives—the world of the Air Age. They are given the idea of circumnavigation of the globe, provided it occurs east-west or west-east. But it does not seem to have come to the attention of their teachers that similar navigation is possible north-south over the poles—and that it revolutionizes our whole way of life.

Fortunately for our hopes for tomorrow, the youngsters have sources of knowledge outside the schoolroom. They gaze into the skies whenever they hear the purring roar of an airplane overhead, and their eyes and ears are keen to catch, and their minds quick to evaluate, the significance of Air Age news. The typically alert boy of twelve or fifteen is today—thanks to knowledge he has gained outside the schoolroom—so much further advanced in matters of global, curved-map geography than are his parents and school-teachers, that he has set a strenuous task for us oldsters to perform before we shall ever have caught up with him.

Maps are not geography. A map is never anything more than a picture of what man thinks at the time when he commits his map to paper. In Homer's day, for example, the world of the map was a flat disc on which sections of dry land surrounded the Mediterranean Sea. About the circumference flowed a boundless body of water which the ancient geographers called the Ocean River, and where it came from or where it went nobody had the slightest idea. Later Ptolemy saw a picture of the world as a wafer with curved edges. A little more land had been found here and there and the Ocean River idea was pretty much discarded, but it was still accepted as axiomatic that you would sail off the edge if you ventured too far. So it went for centuries.

Then came Columbus, and as far as sensible people were concerned, the Genoese who was forever talking about sailing into the West was completely mad. Before he was lucky enough to interest the Queen of Spain in his enterprise, the Republics of Genoa and Venice, the two great maritime powers of the day, had turned down the opportunity to buy into his project. The merchants of Venice and Genoa, judged by today's business standards, were no fools. They owned fleets of ships, built for the carrying trade of the enclosed Mediterranean Sea and the coastal waters of the Atlantic. In the event that Columbus's theories might turn out to be correct, the result would be that the Venctian and Genoese fleets would have to be scrapped and new ships built, capable of sailing the open oceans. That, primarily, was why Columbus encountered so much difficulty in finding backers. In other words, the old geography was too convenient to be discarded in favor of new ideas. Hence the gentlemen of commerce in Genoa and Venice refused to take Columbus seriously, whereas it was comparatively simple to interest Ferdinand and Isabella of Spain, because they were seeking a way to get into maritime trade in a big way and Columbus looked like a good long-odds gamble. So he sailed west and in due course came upon what was later called the New World. (My friend the late Stephen Leacock once said that it was a great mistake to give the gentleman so much credit for his discovery of the Americas, inasmuch as he could not avoid bumping into them somewhere between Hudson Strait and the Straits of Magellan.)

Columbus's discovery immediately brought a new general conception of geography into being according to which the earth was divided naturally into western and eastern land masses separated by vast stretches of water.

Since distances were great and ships not merely slow but at the mercy of wind and sea, nations became collectors of islands in the oceans, places where ships could put in for supplies, fresh water and sanctuary, and were ready to fight to hold these islands at the drop of a belaying pin.

Once more men were convinced they had come to the be-all and end-all of world geography, and that nothing could happen to change it.

Then came the ocean-going steamship which broadened men's concepts and enlarged their freedom. Canals were dug across isthmuses, as at Suez and Panama. Voyages around the Horn and the Cape of Good Hope became more and more rare. Men no longer were at the mercy of the winds. Hence the islands which their storm-tossed sailing ships had visited for refit, water, and provisions became liabilities, not assets, to the nations which owned them. Moreover the discovery had been made that the shortest distance between two points on the world's surface is not a straight line, as it had seemed to be in the earlier conception, but a curved line following the contour of the globe.

Now, instead of mid-ocean islands, what may be called the geographical bottlenecks, of which there were no more than a dozen in the sea-going world, became the valued possessions of the trading nations. For example, a ship could not get into or out of the Indian Ocean without passing the Cape of Good Hope, Southeast Australia, the Strait of Malacca, or the Strait of Bab el Mandeb and the Suez Canal. That meant that Cape Town, Sydney, Singapore, Aden, and Alexandria became places of extreme strategic importance, in which respect it is interesting to note that the British, already the world's greatest sea traders, managed to get hold of all these, as they did with most of the others.

It was through the medium of these great ocean bottlenecks and the tremendous naval strength which Britain developed to control them, that mankind sailed the seas for more than a hundred years under the protection of the "Pax Britannica." It was a traders' world and it was a sea world, but it was still very much a flat world as most people saw it. Moreover, as in Homer's day, in

Ptolemy's and Columbus's, it was a world the geography of which would never change; so everybody, including the seafaring British, staunchly believed. America, convinced that the world's geography had been settled for all time, dreamed of majestic isolation without "foreign entanglements." Its people, regarding the oceans as insurmountable barriers between themselves and any possible invader, assured each other that they could live their own lives without danger of interference from any outside power or powers when, as a matter of fact, their isolation was made possible primarily by the fact that Britain, a friendly sea power, controlled virtually all the strategic bottlenecks and made no attempt to prevent peaceful use of them by her friends. That, perhaps, is neither here nor there. The point in all this is to bring before the reader the concept of the world as it was before the arrival of the Air Age and to impress on him that mankind accepted as axiomatic the view that nothing could happen to change geography again. Then suddenly geography underwent a revolution as great as, if not greater than, that which it experienced on the return of Columbus from the West.

Let us think for just a moment of what happened to the Atlantic Ocean. The *Mayflower* made the crossing in sixty-five days. The first transatlantic steamship reached New York from Britain in fifteen days, cutting the width of the Atlantic by 75 per cent. The *Queen Mary* reduced the width again by almost 75 per cent by shuttling between Sandy Hook and Southampton Water in a matter of four days. Today the crossing is made in less than twenty-four hours by multi-engined aircraft, and the Atlantic has become little more than a millpond. Yet the people of the democracies, most of their statesmen, and even some of their aviation experts still relate the oceans to the geography of the flat map and the tramp steamer.

What has happened to create the new geography of the Air Age?

In preceding paragraphs I have mentioned the great bottlenecks interposed between the oceans and have shown how the seas were dominated by the people who controlled these gateways. The coming of global aviation, while it has not completely destroyed the value of these key points, nevertheless has gone far toward doing so. In order to reach the Far East today, for example, it is not necessary to pass through the Strait of Gibraltar and the Suez Canal. Those who are hostile to the controllers of these gateways can simply fly over them and by-pass them. Conceivably, as the Air Age develops (and I am speaking now in the military sense), it will be possible to move huge forces of men and supplies by air with complete or almost complete disregard for the strategic sea junctions, and to land and maintain invasion forces far behind them. That has happened in some degree in this war. What will happen if ever we find ourselves involved in World War III almost beggars the imagination.

On the day before these lines were written an airplane whisked across the curved map non-stop from the British Isles and landed in Montreal sixteen hours after its take-off in Britain. Five years ago Montreal, the Montreal of the old flat map, though one of the world's great seaports, was icebound and closed for several months in the year. Today, because global aviation has become an accomplished fact and has brought us face to face with the new geography, Montreal is an all year port from which it is possible to travel to anywhere in the world without regard to the conditions of climate which formerly kept its gates tightly closed for almost half of each twelve-month period.

At the commencement of the present war, Moscow was a city which, in the average North American mind, lay somewhere east from New York, across the Atlantic and over the other side of France and Germany. The Moscow of the Air Age is no longer there. Now Moscow is a city reached by flight north from New York around the top of the world via Reykjavik and down on the other side, a matter of a few hours' flying time from any center in the eastern United States or Canada. So it is with all the distant places we used to take endless weeks to reach. Today they are just across the street. The great polar ice barrier has ceased to exist. Now we can be almost anywhere in the world between sun-up and sun-up.

That is what is meant in speaking of "The New Geography." All the old concepts of Eastern and Western Hemispheres, of tremendous ocean barriers behind which we thought we could hide from potential enemies and behind which we believed we could live our own lives in splendid isolation—all these have disappeared. The new geography brings into being a new world. It was created by the airplane and what we do about the new world depends on what we do about aviation, now and tomorrow. Meanwhile men still think in terms of the world they knew during the last interval between wars; the world which placed Russia a full hemisphere away from

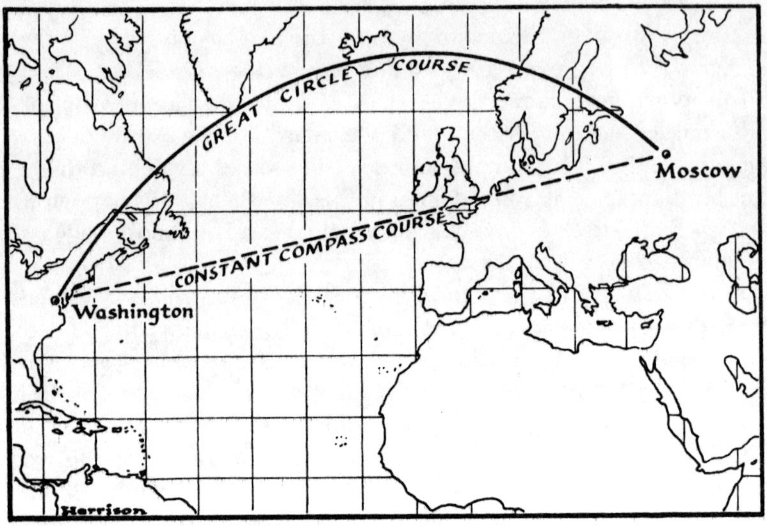

The average person, thinking of the route from Washington to Moscow, would envisage a fortnight's journey eastward—probably from New York to London, from London across the English Channel, and then by rail across Germany, before the border of Russia is crossed—a distance of almost 6000 miles. The time and distance traveled have been made necessary by the facilities of the past; the thought that Northern Europe can be most directly approached by traveling eastward is a misconception based upon the Mercator projection (above) on which the shortest actual route cannot be represented as a straight line save at the equator or in north and south directions. The curved line on this map, which looks longer, actually represents the shortest distance between Washington and Moscow.

America, which thought of Tokyo as a strange place beyond the Pacific, a world in which Africa was still a dark and distant continent.

What will be the impact of the new geography on the life of man? I cannot answer that question completely because I do not know what men are going to do about it. But this much I *do* know: if people living in one part of the world pattern their lives on the new geography and people living in another part of the world fail to do so, then, sooner or later, those who orient themselves to the geography of the Air Age will rule those who fail to do so. I think that puts the matter in a nutshell. At least it should make clear to anyone that the first problem which faces us in our consideration of postwar aviation is not who is going to fly from where to where, and how much money he is going to make by doing so, but how we are going to organize the world to meet the new way of life imposed upon us by this new geography. The airplane created it. The airplane already has revolutionized every concept of life we held when we embarked upon the great adventure of World War II.

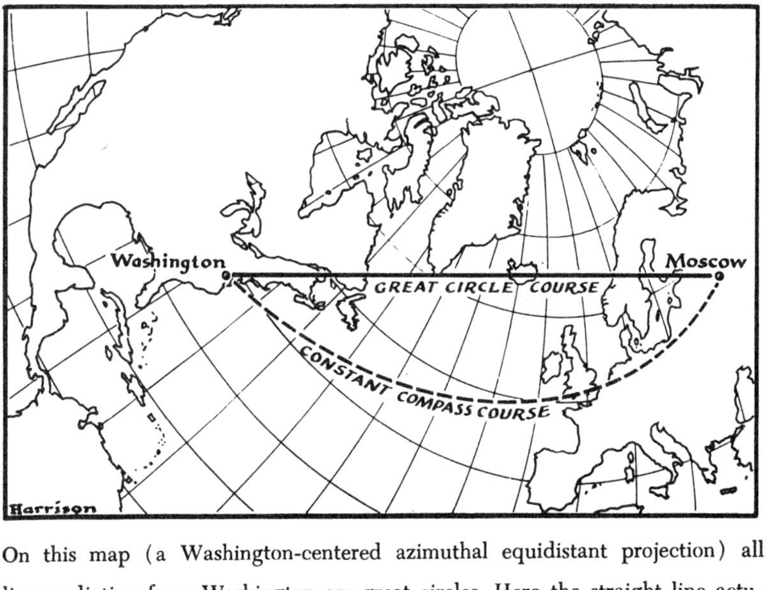

On this map (a Washington-centered azimuthal equidistant projection) all lines radiating from Washington are great circles. Here the straight line actually represents the shortest way to Moscow and shows the route of the Air Age —from Washington northward to Newfoundland, across the tip of Greenland and through Iceland, a distance of less than 5000 miles which can be flown in twenty-three hours—while the old sea and land route is shown by the curved line to be far longer.

CHAPTER 2

What Is the New Map?

WHILE it would probably be oversimplification to say that the United Nations almost lost World War II because they had neglected to study geography, the statement is too close to bald fact to be comfortable. I will enlarge on it by saying that if we do not learn more about the geography of the Air Age than seems to be our inclination at present, we may easily lose the peace and, at no far-distant date, confront mankind with the even greater calamity of World War III.

The long and short of the matter is that North Americans—or perhaps I should say the Western Democracies—have not taken the trouble to ascertain the tremendous implications of flight in its relationship to the new map. It could almost be said that anything we have learned up to this time we have picked up from our enemies. Let me give one brief example of the difference between our approach and that of Germany, one which goes back a great many years, as the history of aviation is measured, but which is still valid. When Blériot made the first Channel flight from France to Britain, English-language newspapers the world over acclaimed the feat as an act of tremendous heroism and daring. The newspapers of Germany, however, took an entirely different view. Blériot's daring left them cold. What intrigued them was that the French aviator had ended the status of the United Kingdom as an island and made it part of the European mainland. That was geopolitics at work—and times have not changed the German outlook.

Geography has always been founded on communication, and geographical knowledge has always increased in ratio to improvements in communication. The Romans invented the hard-surfaced highway and over it carried their culture and conquest to the thithermost parts of the then-known world, "discovering" it and therefore adding to the knowledge of geography. The Mohammedans spread their culture throughout the East through the medium of the horse which, they realized, could carry men great distances and bring Mohammed's influence to other men living far away. Genghis Khan overran half the world because he hit upon the idea of the war-chariot pulled by many horses—the panzer divisions of the early war-like world. North American culture, which had its origin in Western Europe, was brought across the ocean by the sailing vessel and later by the steamship. Continentally, the United States became a great nation, developed its great natural resources, and learned about its own internal geography through the railway and finally the automobile, which robbed local or regional cultures of the isolation they had possessed in ox-cart and horse-and-buggy days and developed the modern American outlook. These things are the very stuff of the science of geography.

What do you think is likely to happen now that man has developed a means of communication which releases him from imprisonment on the surface of the earth, and carries him through the skies over every barrier which yesterday's geography placed in his path? The first objective is that of achieving a world outlook to replace the national and regional approach. The horse and buggy developed purely local geographical cultures. Railway trains and motor cars developed nationalism. Now the airplane makes essential the establishment of *world* culture, a *world* view of the responsibilities of citizenship.

I am not suggesting that regionalism, or regional cultures will disappear entirely because people are now able to move in a hurry from one region to another. Norwegians will still be Norwegians. They will still give loyalty to Norway and be prepared to die to maintain its integrity, if need be. Americans are not going to become Germans or Russians or polyglot. But you cannot create a society in which the peoples of nations hitherto widely separated suddenly establish contacts which may be consummated in a matter of hours without tremendous world repercussions resulting. The Air Age must bring us entirely new concepts of citizenship, of national and international relations. First amongst these must be world-wide acceptance of the oneness of all nations, the indivisibility of peace. If our leaders do not realize this in fabricating the coming peace and in organizing the world beyond victory, mankind is going to be in for a peck of trouble.

Well, we cannot permit ourselves to walk in fear of change, because change is upon us now. The only way to have prevented the coming of the Air Age and its new geography would have been to strangle all the air scientists twenty years ago, before they could emerge from their laboratories with the inventions they have made available to man, and which man is now using. All we can do, therefore, is to accept these phenomena as science continues to make them available and as quickly as possible reorient our way of life, praying the while to whatever gods we profess that we may be able to keep pace with the scientists in our own political development. Most of the troubles we have encountered in trying to create a stable civilization have arisen from the inability of political man to keep pace with the man of science. Scientists fear nothing. They are always ready for anything. Politicians, on the other hand, walk in deadly fear of their own shadows and of those of the people from whom they draw their power.

We have embarked upon two world wars since the turn of the century. We speak of World War I and now of World War II and some people talk about World War III as if it were just around the corner. But it is all one war and it will not end until one of two things happens: either man will destroy the civilization he has worked through the centuries to create (the culminating force of which is global aviation) or he will bring that civilization into control and use its new forces to create a greater and finer civilization. Let us look at the record.

We have never taken the trouble to ascertain what the repeated clash with Germany is fundamentally about. But Germany knows. She knew in 1914 and she knew in 1939. In 1914 Germany set upon us because we were in control of the sea highways, through the medium of British control of the inter-ocean bottlenecks. Germany launched her thunderbolts against the world again in 1939 because she believed she could gain a world-wide advantage through air-power before the rest of us were alive to its implications. But let us go back to World War I for a moment.

The German plan, we know now, was to crush Russia and France and make the German people masters of Europe. Then she would have made use of all the ship-building potential of the Continent to challenge and destroy British and American sea-power and acquire complete domination of the oceans of the world.

Very few people realized it at the time, or even later. Certainly none of the world's isolationists did—and most of us became isolationists as soon as World War I was over, if we had not been so before. In the United States from 1914 to 1917, for example, most people regarded what was going on beyond the Atlantic as a purely European squabble, and Uncle Sam finally became enraged because the Germans would not leave American shipping alone. When they finally declared war, the American people did so as if it were their own private war and not one in which they were engaging as anybody's ally. They were joining in as "isolated Americans" whose business had been tampered with by Germany, not as partners in a world-wide social conflict.

Virtually the same thing happened in World War II. The power of isolationist elements in the United States (and before them that of Europe's appeasers, which is simply another name for sufferers from geopolitical blindness) was so great in the beginning that the few leaders who visualized the conflict as global, and as a direct threat to the freedom of the world, including that of the continental United States itself, dared not issue a call to arms in defiance of a public opinion which insisted on looking inward when it should have been looking outward. They were not able to do so until Japan saved the life of America by bombing Pearl Harbor. It is eminently doubtful if many free men know to this day what they are really fighting for or against, choosing to believe the war is for national, not global, survival.

But back to World War I. The original Allies, plus the United States, succeeded in beating the Central powers to their knees. As soon as that was done, however, the American people withdrew to their cave in the Western Hemisphere and refused to have anything to do with the idea of world security or world organization. That was simply because their leaders had never taken the trouble to instill the rudiments of political geography into their people or even to learn geography themselves. The result was that the great majority of Americans came to believe that they had sent their young men across the Atlantic to "rescue" France and Britain, whose motives soon were painted as by no means altruistic (possibly a correct assumption). Soon the opposition to the League of Nations, which began as a domestic political *putsch* to "get Wilson," reached new proportions and, finally, touched the nadir of almost 100 per cent isolationism. Without doubt many Americans were completely idealistic in their isolationist views. Their republic had been founded on isolationism, on a determination to escape from the bondage of the Old World to fashion a completely independent nation in the new.

Washington and Jefferson were isolationists in a day when isolationism was almost synonymous with liberalism. Many isolationists of the between-wars years, therefore, were merely following the dictates of conscience and upbringing, true to the doctrines of some of the greatest of their founding fathers.

So the greatest power in the Western Hemisphere withdrew from effective political association with the rest of mankind, a seclusion maintained for more than twenty years. Remembering that we were still living in the sea world when World War I ended, I do not think it an exaggeration to say that America convinced herself that so long as she remained behind her ocean barriers no harm could come to her. We know now that the assumption was entirely wrong. It was wrong in a sea-power world. In the Air Age any such assumption is suicidal folly. The airplane has destroyed isolationism forever.

Germany and her associates came within a whisker of winning the First World War, thanks to her use of the submarine, the only weapon with which an inferior sea power could attack a superior one. Her failure was in large measure due to the fact that Germany's U-boats could not destroy enough Allied shipping quickly enough. Otherwise the free peoples were doomed, even in a sea-power war. World War II has been waged on Germany's new assumption that air-power, supporting mechanized land forces and attacking shipping at sea in conjunction with the submarine, is invulnerable. We shall succeed in turning back the challenge again, but I do not believe that we can continue forever to accept these challenges. Sooner or later, if the practice continues, we shall lose a war, and with it our freedom. Not forever can we hope to win through a combination of the courage of our young men, the productivity of our industries, and the help of God Almighty. I think some of our military leaders, and certainly many of those who lead in the field of aviation, are fully alive to the factors at work. But I am not sure that many of our statesmen are and I am positive that our populations as a whole are not. How can they be? No intelligent instruction has been given them. By no means all the young men who fly from the Pacific Coast of the United States to Australia, or from Montreal to Karachi, know what is happening. They simply have jobs to do and are doing them to the best of their skill, ingenuity, and courage. Most people (and I include a great many political gentlemen, particularly those who still think that the most important thing in life is to be re-elected from a given Congressional District, or to the Canadian Parliament from a constituency in Ontario) are still thinking of the airplane solely as a weapon of war, or as a means of commercial communication capable of covering long east-west distances as shown on the old rectangular map.

Well, it is neither. If the airplane is regarded primarily as a weapon its ultimate use will be destruction. Commercially the airplane has not simply made it possible to get from one place to another over the old routes, but to its own new dimension it has added the new global geography, taking that geography into partnership and flying its traffic lanes to shrink the world to a tenth of its prewar size. If we fail to shape what has happened for the good of all men new troubles lie ahead. That is a point I shall discuss at length as we go along. Here I am concerned solely with driving home the facts of life as they are contained for all of us between the covers of the geography of the Air Age.

CHAPTER 3

Design for Conquest

AFTER Germany had been defeated in 1918 the Allies set about dismembering her for the purpose of making her too weak to fight for long years to come. Bits and pieces of country rich in natural resources, but largely inhabited by Germans, became parts of Czechoslovakia and Poland. Austria was given its independence. Danzig, Memel, and the Saar were mandated to the League of Nations. The Allies occupied the Ruhr and gave Malmédy and Eupen to Belgium, another area to Italy, and annexed Alsace-Lorraine to France, including even those sections which are preponderantly German. At the same time we took Germany's navy away from her, disbanded her army, seized her colonies, and convinced ourselves that we had so weakened our enemies that never again would they be able to rise against us. In which way of thinking we counted without the spirit of a consistently war-like and ambitious people and at the same time completely neglected to put curbs on the selfishness of greedy traders in our own ranks who soon would be establishing cartel arrangements with our industrially and scientifically brilliant erstwhile enemies.

Almost before the ink was dry on the Treaty of Versailles, Germany's geographers were trying to ascertain why the Reich had lost the war and laying plans to win the next one. As a first step they organized a great geographical research institute to explore the problem and find a solution. While the educators of the democracies continued to teach the young the bare rudiments of flat geography and discontinued even this elementary procedure when the child left the primary school, the Germans were making home geography, world geography, and geopolitics the hubs about which their whole educational system from kindergarten to university—and indeed their entire national life—revolved.

The story of Germany's renaissance during the postwar years needs no retelling. Even before Hitler came to power, the Reich was making ready for a new war of conquest by conserving her own resources, developing substitutes for those she lacked, creating great new industries, acquiring enormous stocks of materials from the outside world, mobilizing her entire population to work for the Fatherland, and finally, leading the whole world in the development of aviation—all with our assistance.

Industrialists and financiers in the democracies saw in association with Germany the possibility of profitable trade and gave no thought to the uses to which the goods they sold would be put. Hence the great intercontinental cartels, presently under the fire of liberal political leaders. In other words, some of our own people, in their blindness to the nature of the German plan, assisted our enemies to prepare for a new war. That they should do so and that democratic political leaders encouraged them, clearly indicates that we knew nothing of the world's political geography and still believed that oceans are fortifications which render us impregnable even to the extent of making it "safe" to sell the matériel of war to those who await only the opportunity to strike us down. No more fallacious idea ever governed the thinking of otherwise intelligent people.

The next great step toward German re-establishment came through her correct assumption that little difficulty would be encountered in attempting to tear up the Treaty of Versailles for the purpose of reuniting the German peoples in Middle Europe. In this ambition Germany found a sympathetic ear at her disposal in high places, because, with the war forgotten, reasonable men guilelessly accepted the thesis that members of the German family could not be blamed for all wanting to live under the same roof. Soon, however, the Germans showed their hand by letting it be seen that their ideas of a greater Germany did not begin and end with the repatriation of Germans living outside the border of the Reich, but that the true objective was to obtain military resources. You know what happened then—the democracies launched the policy of Appeasement, because they wanted to trade, not fight. Finally even the 100 per cent Appeasers in Britain and France realized that the game could not go on. Already Austria had been absorbed and Czechoslovakia overrun. Now pledges were given to Poland and when the Germans poured their air armadas across the borders Britain and France declared war. Poland fell in three weeks. She fell, not because her people refused to fight, but because Germany thrust five great mechanized spearheads, operating under a canopy of airplanes which virtually blackened the skies, against an unprepared nation. That was the physical beginning of World War II. Actually it had begun on the day when Germany's political geographers began to ask each other why World War I had been lost, while we blandly assumed that the bucklers and bastions of other days still were valid defenses.

The war went on. Britain and France still believed that a combination of naval blockade and the Maginot defenses, which ended in the air at the Franco-Belgian border, ultimately would enable us to starve Germany out. Suddenly the Germans moved into Denmark and the conquest of that neutral country was effected by the simple process of occupying its airfields. Then Germany darted across the Kattegat and the Skagerrak under the widely spread umbrella of the *Luftwaffe* and Norway was occupied. The Royal Navy had to withdraw from that engagement because it had no parasol over its head. Then came Holland. The Dutch cut their dikes and flooded their country, so the Germans simply flew over the flooded area and conquered Holland's cities from the air. So too with Belgium, where the German air force, covering the *Wehrmacht,* reduced another gallant but unprepared nation to pulp in a matter of days. France came next and France in turn was conquered because she had been thinking in national, or regional, geographical terms and had made no preparation for the type of warfare her conquerors launched. Again, it was the *Luftwaffe* cloud, covering the spearheads of the ground forces, which rolled over a helpless people who had pinned their hopes on ground fortresses and were virtually without aerial defense. Fortunately for the British (and I would like to remind all good democrats again of our tendency to rely on the help of God Almighty when our enemies assail us) heavy fogs in the English Channel saved the Expeditionary Forces from annihilation and enabled the greater part of it to escape from Dunkirk aboard a nondescript fleet of small naval craft, tugs, fishing boats, motor launches, pleasure steamers, and every imaginable sort of conveyance capable of moving over the water. It was one of the greatest examples of human heroism in all the grandeur of arms. But its roots were embedded in the stupidity of leaders whose eyes were blind to a changing world. Germany's drive to the West had been successful.

Now the Nazi horde turned southeast and occupied the north coast of Africa by ferrying a huge army and its mechanized equipment across the Mediterranean under a dense air blanket. Once again

German air-power had enabled her to by-pass the bottlenecks. She drove into the Balkans and quickly crushed organized resistance in Yugoslavia by bombing its cities into rubble. German dive-bombers drove us out of Greece and we retreated in ships to the island of Crete, where the Germans descended on us by parachute and glider and again we had to make our escape over the water—because we were still living in the Sea Age and had allowed the coming of the Air Age to catch us napping. So goes the grim story of Germany's subjugation of western and southern Europe, spearheaded by the airplane.

No change of tactics or strategy occurred when the Nazis turned on Russia. Again the series of ground-borne spearheads drove forward under a blanket of aircraft. The Western powers still assumed that the whole German strategy related solely to the conquest of the Eurasian land mass. Isolationists in the Americas still called it a European squabble, an imperialist brawl, but never the first round of a death struggle for world domination. When Mussolini's legions moved into the French Riviera they saw it only as a "stab in the back" of helpless France, not as part of a closely knit plan of world conquest. I am quite sure that when the United States was bombed into the war at Pearl Harbor, the American people were convinced, as many of them still are, that the bestial Japanese were simply taking advantage of the existing preoccupations of the Western Democracies to wrest for themselves new power in the Pacific, possibly to deflect American aid from the nations involved in the "shooting war." Nothing could be further from the truth. Every act of aggression of our enemies has been part of their over-all plan of world conquest and, as such, has been closely integrated with every other move, no matter in what part of the world it has taken place. Thus the Japanese attack on Pearl Harbor was simply one facet of the plan designed in Germany by the Hitler geographers, part of the master plan of world conquest, and it was made when Hitler gave the signal. What was the plan?

After disabling the United States Pacific fleet, Japan would move huge armies southward over the sea, under the protection of great air-power, conquering the Orient, then quickly turning west to overrun Burma and India. Meanwhile Germany would drive east through South Russia, across the Black Sea and through Turkey to Iraq, where the Japanese and Germans were to meet by fixed appointment. Success of this phase of the plan would have resulted in driving the British out of the Indian Ocean. It came close to succeeding. But for Russia's continued resistance, it would probably have done so. Meanwhile Japan, deploying other forces into Eastern Siberia, was to cut Russia off from supplies from the American continent through her Siberian entry. In the meantime the blockading of Murmansk would have cut off the Soviets' Atlantic supply route. If complete success had attended this program, as it nearly did, Russia and China would soon have been choked into submission.

Let me stress here for the benefit of those North Americans who insist on regarding Japan as their Number I Enemy, that the senior partner in all this enterprise was, is, and always will be Germany. Japan and Italy were never more than satellites fighting for the German geo-planners. Had the German master plan been able to maintain its timetable, it would have given the Axis so great an industrial potential that its members could have taken their own good time to polish off the Americas. The partners would have enjoyed a superabundance of natural resources to build up inexhaustible heavy war industries. Endless streams of oil would have flowed to their refineries and from them to airfields, naval bases, and military establishments. Virtually all the world's rubber would have been in their possession. If Britain had not already been overwhelmed it would have been no trick to knock her out of the war by air and seaborne invasions, or perhaps by the less costly device of starving her. Africa would have become an Axis continent and the Germans would have been looking across the narrow waters of the South Atlantic from Dakar, ready to pounce on the Americas at the opportune moment. The Japanese, of course, would have been in Australia by this time and Germany's air arm would have subjugated the northern stepping stones to America, Iceland, and Greenland. So went the master plan. If time were needed to prepare for the final phase, the subjugation of America, it could be secured through a negotiated peace.

If it is necessary to present any further evidence to establish our blindness to Axis infiltration, let me point out that the ground work for the attack upon the United States and Canada already had been laid in South America (discussed in a later chapter) where the work of preparing for conquest was going full blast. If it is necessary to point out even more strongly the geographical blindness of our people, let me refer you to the policies of appeasement in which we persisted in South America, choosing to act as if political manifestations in the Argentine were none of our business while the obvious and fully known policies of those who governed that country constituted direct threats to the safety of the North American continent and to our whole free way of life. No doubt, had the Germans been successful, we should have come alive to the real implications of world conquest by the time the war had reached the phase at which Germany could have taken full advantage of its South American infiltration, but by then it would have been too late. The Germans and their satellites would have been poised to strike and their power would have been invincible. They would strike from South America while the Japanese moved with massed airplane carriers from the Pacific islands and other forces descended upon us from the north through Alaska. Another great German air armada would have leap-frogged through Iceland and Greenland to attack our northeast coast. The United States and Canada would then become the final battlefield and the scene of the greatest and bloodiest drama in the history of mankind.

That is what our enemies had planned. To you who read these pages, steeped as you have been in ideas of security which have been solely continental, it will have all the qualities of a nightmare the victim of which awakens and soon is laughing at his own fears.

That is because we still accept the flat-map geography which gives rise to the smug conclusion that "it-can't-happen-here." Our weird beliefs have direct relationship to the fervent North American idea that we are impregnable behind our ocean barriers, and its corollary which holds that one North American can lick his weight in wildcats. Perhaps he can when he is better armed than the wildcats. If he is not, the wildcats ultimately are going to win a war. If the wildcats are so fortunate as to arrive by airplane and parachute while others crash through our doors simultaneously from the sea, then it is not going to be much help to be standing firm in mid-continental Kansas City or Des Moines without a gun.

Such was the Axis program of conquest. Fortunately it encountered unforeseen resistances which set back the timetable. Thank God Hitler blundered. Thank God he underestimated the common people of Britain and Russia! That was our good fortune, not the result of our good sense. The German plan was a plan for world conquest, nothing else. It was a plan founded on a knowledge of geography and one which took advantage of geography and its development as a science in the global Air Age.

PART II

Wings and the Man

CHAPTER 1

In the Beginning

ALONG with our failure to see the Air Age in focus as it has unfolded before our eyes—or, if we saw it, to act upon our knowledge—there has lurked in men's minds the ineradicable fallacy that the final phase of aviation's development and utility has always just been reached. Here is a means of human communication and a weapon of human destruction which functions in a new element, the air, and which has added a new dimension, depth (or height, if you prefer the term) to our world.

When the first flights of a few moments' duration took place, most people saw nothing to these feats but what may be called their "stunt" quality. When the air scientists of World War I developed aircraft capable of wreaking havoc upon the enemy, the politician onlooker saw nothing but a new and minor weapon restricted in its use to short ranges. When the oceans were first crossed by air, we acclaimed these successes solely as testimony to the pioneering spirit of our young aviators, not as the impending dawn of global flight. When airlines expanded across the seven seas we were sure aviation at last had reached its peak, that all we could add would be the occasional amenity for the traveler. We remained sure that air routes would never be able to compete with those which lie on the surface of the sea. We were, in short, the twentieth-century replicas of those maritime merchants of Genoa and Venice who laughed Columbus out of court when he announced his intention of discovering a westward passage to the East. As our transocean airlines have been increased a thousandfold under the impact of World War II, most people have chosen to regard what has happened as a development which will be laid aside as soon as Peace breaks out again. To the average democrat and his political leaders the mass-bombings of our enemies' fortresses and cities mark the final stage of the use of the airplane as a weapon. It is final in exactly the same sense that a pocket-dagger is as great as a cavalryman's saber. When such people read about rockets and jets they jeer again, simply because their minds cannot be projected beyond the power capacities of the stationary engine. We have been, in short (and this goes for all of us, on the democratic side, at least), a pack of stupid fools.

There is only one way to bring home the possibilities inherent in the immediate future. That is to survey the whole course of aviation's history. We must turn back, then, and see what has happened —how aviation began and how it was received by "solid men of sense"; how it surged forward under the tremendous impact of the first war in the air; its gigantic development in spite of the political imposts placed upon it between two wars; and, finally, its second great forward surge under the shattering driving power of a second world war.

A great deal has been written in the past about the pioneers of flight, of the struggles of the brothers Wright and the belittling of their effort, as derision is always showered on the heads of innovators by hidebound and ignorant people who walk in terror of change because they fear the adjustments they may have to make to meet it. Those were the days of Blériot, Graham-White, de Lesseps, and all the band of gallant pioneers who ventured into the new element, the air, in contraptions which looked like strange bugs mounted on bicycle wheels. The story of Orville and Wilbur Wright is part of every American boy's folklore. So is the legendry of Santos-Dumont and others to the European.

In my own country, Canada, where the first flight ever made from British soil began and finished at Baddeck, N.S., on February 23, 1909, a young gaffer, J. A. D. McCurdy, took off from and landed on the frozen surface of one of the Bras d'Or Lakes in a funny-looking equipage called the *Silver Dart.* I can think of no better way of calling attention to the extreme youth of flight than by saying that this same young man, the first to fly in the British Empire, as this is written is still involved in aviation as one of the high officials of the Air Production Branch of Canada's Department of Munitions and Supply, which has equipped our mammoth Air Training Plan with the aircraft in which tens of thousands of young Canadians, Americans, Englishmen, Australians, New Zealanders, Poles, Hollanders, Czechs, and Fighting Frenchmen have learned to fly, and from the schools of which they have gone forth to knock the Hun out of the skies and to bomb his cities into heaps of rubble. In other words, aviation's whole lusty history has been recorded within the memory of men still alive and active, which stresses not merely the extreme youth of aviation itself, but the speed of the world revolution it has caused. Like all youngsters it has always been up to something its elders look upon with distrust, disapproval, and sometimes scorn. Like all youngsters it has made great mistakes, usually owing to youth's lack of judgment. But, like the young everywhere, it is up and coming, always going places, and full of the spirit of never-say-die, and we cannot hold it back simply by telling it to behave.

I would give a lot to have been with McCurdy and his friends on the ice at Baddeck that February day. Probably none of those present realized that history was being written, but what was set down that morning was the opening paragraph of one of the most important chapters of Canadian and aviation history. That was the day when all the great Canadian pilots of World War I were born. and it was the day when the huge Canadian bases from which men now fly over the new map to India, Africa, Burma, to anywhere in the world, were first conceived in the spirit of high adventure.

Like the Wright brothers, the gentlemen whose money, plans, and determination made the flight of *Silver Dart* possible had their troubles. As far as the residents of the immediate vicinity were concerned, the innovators were all lunatics who would undoubtedly break their necks and richly deserved to do so for daring to attempt to override the purposes of the Almighty. As was true of aerial experimenters everywhere in the world, they could not have taken a single dollar away from any so-called responsible citizen to further their strange and God-defying purpose. But, like pioneers everywhere, they went ahead anyway.

They had begun to tinker with their great idea two years earlier. Its principal backer was Dr. Alexander Graham Bell, inventor of the telephone, and he was actually only backer-by-proxy, in that he had managed to persuade Mrs. Bell to let him and his associates have $35,000 with which to build their first flying machine. The associates called themselves the Aerial Experiment Association and one of their number was the great Glenn Curtiss, the others being Dr. Bell (then living at Baddeck), Thomas Selfridge, J. A. D. McCurdy, and a renowned Canadian character by the name of Casey Baldwin. Almost two years elapsed between the day when Dr. Bell persuaded his wife to write a check and the great moment when *Silver Dart* took off to the dismay and chagrin of the scoffers.

I have spent a great deal of time since I became associated with aviation wondering how McCurdy ever managed to climb up from the ice and seat himself in the *Silver Dart*. Sometimes nowadays I hear people wondering aloud how the young pilots of today ever manage to squeeze themselves into the cockpit with all the gear and gadgets they wear, from parachute packs to Mae Wests, but to me their problem looks like child's play compared to the one which faced McCurdy, for, as I look at the snapshots of the skintight trousers he wore that morning, I persistently wonder how he could lift a foot six inches above the ground or, having climbed up to the level of the wings, could have managed to assume a sitting position without bursting his seams. That in itself was a great pioneering enterprise and, as far as I am concerned, just another of those things which constantly call attention to the undying courage of our intrepid flying men.

Meanwhile all the backers of the enterprise stood closely huddled together on the ice, some wearing beards and others mustaches which looked like bicycle handle-bars. They were sticking together for the identical reason for which children huddle in the dark, for the comfort and spiritual sustenance they could draw from each other in a world in which everybody else thought they were totally crazy. Finally McCurdy broke away from the group and walked out to the strange contraption he was about to take up into the air. About that time, I am credibly informed, some of the more serious burghers present had it in mind to gang the young man to keep him from committing suicide, or from interfering with what they probably would have described as God's will. Probably because they were not unanimous as to how this should be done, or lacked leadership, the idea was not put into effect. McCurdy climbed up, managed to sit down without tearing his pants, tied himself to the machine, and was ready for the great adventure. *Silver Dart* rolled slowly along the ice. The young man at the controls waved to his partners. The machine picked up speed and took a hop, skip, and jump, while everybody held his breath. Miracle of miracles, it took to the air!

McCurdy flew straight along over the lake for a matter of minutes which must have felt like years. All those who have ever soloed and enjoyed that tremendous sinking feeling in the pit of the stomach followed by the greatest sense of exhilaration man will ever know, will have some idea as to what was going on inside

McCurdy about that time. But this was no ordinary first solo. It was the first solo ever performed from Canadian soil, or in the British Empire, and one of the first performed anywhere.

The great question mark in everybody's mind (including McCurdy's, no doubt) now became how he could get back to the ground without breaking his young neck, which some of the more cynical unbelievers below no doubt secretly hoped he would do, simply as a means of bearing out their conviction and assertion that what was going on constituted something pretty close to mortal sin. There was an audible crowd-gasp as the pilot went into a turn and began to fly in the other direction. *Silver Dart* flew gently and slowly along, continued to frustrate the fundamentalists by not falling to pieces in the air, turned again, glided gently downward toward the lake, and landed softly on its surface. That was the beginning of flight in a country which, for the size of its population, has produced more flying men than any nation on the green footstool, which pioneered the use of aircraft in opening up undeveloped hinterlands, a country which is the home of the most air-minded race on earth.

Such were the beginnings of aviation.

Not much happened during the years which preceded World War I. The designers—men like the Wrights and Santos-Dumont—had to build their own machines with what little money they could scrape together. Every now and then some hardy madman pulled off some new glittering stunt. The London *Daily Mail* dangled a huge cash prize before the eyes of anyone who could span the English Channel by air and Blériot collected. On December 18, 1910, T. O. M. Sopwith, whose name has been closely identified with British aviation in two wars, flew from Eastchurch in Kent to Tirlement, Belgium, a matter of 161 miles. The world acclaimed the feat. Today there are plenty of young Spitfire and Fortress pilots who would have almost as much money as Blériot won if they were given a ten-shilling note for every time they have crossed the Straits of Dover to do the chores of the United Nations' war in the air.

Certainly, when World War I came along, aviation showed little improvement over the planes of Wright, Blériot, and McCurdy. Only a handful of machines were available in England or France when the shooting started. The pilots of that day were sportsmen, leaning a little toward madness, and there was no knowledge in any of them of what may be termed military flight, or of the possibilities of using aircraft as weapons of war. Airplanes were not armed. If they had any use at all it was that of being able to get up where horizons are wider, to observe the course of events below, and to come back to tell the military gentlemen what was going on. The military gentlemen, from all I have ever heard, did not think much of this. It constituted a definite interference with the running of the war by people who had spent their lives learning how to run wars (with Napoleon and Wellington as their mentors), and they wanted no innovators butting into an honorable profession. So the aviators took off and observed and came back and every once in a while one of them brought home valuable information which enabled the military men, albeit unwillingly, to confound the enemy. At that time nobody had fired a shot from one airplane toward another. The machines in use were rickety death-traps tied together with what the latter-day pilot usually speaks of contemptuously as haywire, and not even the most serious-minded survivor of that era will ever deny that both he and his machine *were* completely haywire, in the cynical sense in which the term is used in North American idiom. Probably that is how the phrase found its way into the language.

The first armament ever carried by the fliers of World War I seems to have been the short Lee Enfield rifle and it was carried by some unsung sprat who thought it a good idea to smuggle a gun into the cockpit and surprise the first Jerry he met by taking a potshot at him. So far as I have heard, nobody was ever hurt by it. But it was the birth of a world-shaking idea, which has since resulted in the pouring down of death and destruction on German cities, and the highly skilled trade of aerial combat.

Before the war was many months old, however, all sorts of revolutionary events had taken place. The most important of these, without question, was that the first groups of scientific aircraft designers to be equipped with tools and ample money had locked themselves away from the sight of man and were working day and night, in Germany as in France and Britain, to evolve airplanes which would fly more efficiently and faster, and which could be utilized as weapons of war. Paralleling this activity was the tremendous interest of youngsters who had just donned the uniform in this great new arm of warfare. *They* could see its possibilities even if the generals could not.

We had strange reasons for joining, we kids who were amongst the early members of the old Royal Flying Corps. Take myself. I had crossed from Canada to England as a Cavalry Lieutenant, and by the time I had been there a month it seemed to me I had never seen anything but mud. I would stand fetlock deep in it in the horse lines looking up as the occasional airplane passed overhead, saying to myself, "What a grand clean way to go to war." Right then I decided to find out how a man went about the business of getting away from horses, baled hay, and mud—in short, how he acquired wings. But nobody I met in camp seemed to know anything about it. Then I went up to London for a weekend, and somewhere in the West End (it must have been the Savoy Bar because that was the place to which we all gravitated as soon as we hit town, and, therefore, the place to run into your friends or to hear on the Canadian grapevine who might be around) I ran into a couple of Englishmen who had recently joined the Royal Flying Corps. In the course of our conversation, I learned that if you applied to be sent to the Royal Flying Corps, and you had the necessary qualifications, your senior officers could not block the move. I asked them how to make the applications and the answer staggered me. It was to go direct to the War Office and see Lord Hugh Cecil. If he approved, the transfer would be made. This was Saturday night.

With great fear I went A.W.O.L. on Monday, staying over in London, as broke as any junior officer is in honor bound to be after a weekend in town. Early on Monday morning I advanced timidly into the front door of the War Office in Whitehall. After a short delay, I was led through the rabbit warren it was, and eventually arrived at a very small office where sat Lord Hugh in solitary majesty.

I explained to him that, although I was a trained cavalryman with three years' experience prior to the war, it was my desire to get into the Royal Flying Corps and told him of my conversation with the two young Englishmen. He could not have been more kind, and immediately took down in longhand, on an ordinary scratch-pad, my name, rank, regiment, and other vital statistics. My knowledge of the air was, as I have previously said, just one of youthful dreams born of the sight of a few airplanes passing over our muddy outdoor stables. Actually in my heart I was probably horrified by the thought of flying, but, even so, anything seemed better than the mud in which I was bogged down.

It was a major decision I faced, and I was as nervous as a kitten. Looking back from here, the conversation had qualities of divine comedy.

The questions Lord Hugh asked became more and more frightening as I visualized in my imagination the dreadful things that must happen to people who fly. First, he asked me if I could ride a horse. That was easy. I replied that I had been in a Cavalry Regiment for several years. Point one for Bishop. Then he asked if I could "she." This being the English idea of how to pronounce the word "ski" (for the same reason that Cholmondeley is called "Chumley," no doubt), I had no idea what he meant, unless it had something to do with sex. I played safe and simply answered, "Yes, sir." I got away with that one. Point two. The next question was how well I could drive a motor car. Never having had a wheel in my hand I simply replied, "Very well." Could I ride a motor bike? Again the answer was yes. Then, "How well can you skate?" At last a question I could answer truthfully. Any young Canadian who can't skate and play ice-hockey should be shot. Then Lord Hugh wanted to know if I had done any running, if I had any experience on the track. By this time I had all the answers, simply by couching them in the affirmative. I told him of the many races and cups I had won. After all he'd have to go a long way from Whitehall to check up on me!

In the meantime, I was wondering: What sort of a game *is* this flying anyway? Am I going to land on the lakes of Switzerland, or high in the Alps? Am I going to be chased by battalions of German Infantry, diving in and out of canals, or what? Where was the flying to come in?

To this day I have no idea what the destination of Lord Hugh's cross-examination was. I can only believe his examination stemmed from the belief that you must ask the candidate *something,* if only to impress the young man with the importance of the occasion and that, having no dossier on flight statistics on which to base a questionnaire, Lord Hugh was simply doing what he could to make the occasion seem important.

Finally he pointed out that there were two classes of air crew, pilots and a new type just coming in, to be called "observer," and that it would be easier to join as an observer than as a pilot, as the need was great and I would get to France more quickly.

By this time I was so afraid of flying that I felt I would sooner trust somebody else to pilot the aircraft than do it myself, so I said quickly, "I'd like to be an observer, sir." That is how I went into the Royal Flying Corps. All very scientific!

In a matter of days, after returning to my regiment in Kent, my transfer came through and I reported to Salisbury Plain, there to join the first class of embryo observers and to discover that I was one of the few Canadians in the whole R.F.C., a fellow with an accent and a language which baffled his comrades. They were grand fellows for all their strange ways, and in those days I formed friendships which will never die. That is youth's genius in wars—and the only good that comes of them.

Our training was not quite what the boys of today would call training. Those were the first days of the use of wireless by airmen—and by wireless, I mean something far different from the science today's fliers know. We had small Morse transmitting sets in our machines with which we could send to the ground for a very short distance, while carrying out artillery observation and directing the guns on their targets. The only answer we could receive upstairs from the gunners was given by means of strips of cotton laid on the ground, each of which had a cryptic meaning of its own. It was not until the war was almost over that telephonic communication between the air and the ground was introduced. I well remember being present, in the autumn of 1917 at Dayton, Ohio, while home on leave, when Henry Ford gave the first demonstration in the United States.

To return to the training we had as observers, I always recall that none of us was so hot with our Morse. No wonder. We were sent off every afternoon with huge searchlights, and, on arrival in a field, divided into two groups which were established about a thousand yards apart on the level plain. The procedure was always identical. We memorized our messages before we went out, sent them to the other fellows while an instructor watched and checked. They were always correct, of course. Then he would leave us, with instructions to practice. Whereupon we would find the nearest haystack and sit chatting and dozing behind it while one member of each team kept flashing the lights to convince any "spy" that we were busy. However, some way or other we learned a soupçon of Morse.

After a brief course, in which no flying was done, my class received the single wing which denoted our status. The baker's dozen of us who were graduated became the first observers ever known in the honorable annals of flight. Of aviation we knew nothing, but we were going to find out very quickly. A few days later we were on our way to France (being fliers we went by water, of course), and I was en route to the great adventure of adventures. It was still 1915. The war in the air was just beginning. Thenceforward I was to sit in a ringside seat and watch the science of flight grow from the infant it then was into the giant it has since become.

CHAPTER 2

The Fledgling Fighter Takes to the Air

ON GOING to the front in France at the end of 1915, I joined No. 21 Squadron of the Royal Flying Corps, then equipped with a strange flying contraption known as the RE7 (Reconnaissance Experimental No. 7), a machine designed to mount guns and cameras, a 500-pound bomb lashed to the fuselage, and all manner of other equipment for light aerial housekeeping. The idea was excellent. You would fly to the target, take a quick look over the side of the cockpit, pull a wire cable—and away the bomb would go. Shades of the Norden bombsight! All that was wrong with this was that the machine stoutly refused to leave the ground when all this gear, plus pilot and observer, had been loaded into it.

I remember well the first time we tried it. We gunned across our own airdrome at least a dozen times, trying to get off into the wind, then taxied back to try again, before anyone realized that we were asking too much of the aircraft. Consultation between senior officers followed and it was decided to move to the larger field at St. Omer, 10 miles away, in the hope that with a longer run the RE7 might consent to struggle into the air. Before this decision was taken we had even tried to take off without the bomb and failed.

So the young observer and four machine guns were ferried to St. Omer by truck, while the pilot brought the RE7 across country minus its bomb. At St. Omer, with myself and four Lewis guns added, we got off, the guns being mounted on four pegs on the forward cockpit rim. The bomb was simply left behind, since the plane utterly refused to lift it.

It will always remain a question of reasonable doubt whether anybody could have fired the guns at an enemy. To have done so would have entailed possessing the eye of a sharpshooter and the agility of an acrobat, because to fire a bullet into the clear you first had to shoot through the maze of wires between the upper and lower wings, which gave the RE7 the appearance of a bird cage. But the bird cage got into the air, although hours must have elapsed as we circled around and around St. Omer until we had attained an altitude of 6000 feet and could set off toward the lines. There I had my first taste of ack-ack fire and I remember it was hard to take, though later I felt completely a hero for having come through this visit to the baptismal font of war. True, it was nothing like the anti-aircraft fire today's fliers endure. Its shooting was done by fallible human beings, not by scientific range-finding devices. But it was just as hard to take, for remember our machines were not so good either.

Ack-ack or no ack-ack, however, we slipped across the enemy lines, visited the German batteries, the positions of which the artillery wanted to tape down, took photographs (praying the while nobody would catch us at it and want to discuss the matter), and sneaked home. That was my introduction to war in the air, and I imagine it corresponded closely to that of every other old-time observer.

Fully loaded, the top speed of the RE7 was 60 miles an hour and it stalled at 48, so you can well imagine what little climbing you could do in one, or for that matter, any other kind of maneuvering. The instrument panel—only a little less simple than that of an automobile—provided the pilot with almost no information beyond an erratic guess as to his altitude. When a pilot wanted to change direction left or right, or up or down, he had to *throw* the stick in the direction in which he wanted to go; not just touch it with a finger, but really slam it around. Putting on rudder was done about as gently as throwing out the clutch of an old-fashioned automobile. The things were nearly as maneuverable as 10-ton trucks, but by no means as safe. Pilots who failed to break their necks by stalling and spinning into the ground were sitting ducks for any land-bound soldier with an anti-aircraft gun and one good eye. So the powers brought us back from the line and gave us the job of providing aerial defense for General Sir Douglas Haig's headquarters at St. Omer. Day in and out, in the freezing mist of a Pas de Calais February, we beetled over headquarters and the adjoining town. Fortunately the enemy did not seem to know we were there, for what we could have done to defend the place I do not know. Presumably we would have tried to join issue with the Hun if he had come along and, I imagine, have been shot down ingloriously for our pains, for even then the gentleman could outmatch us in the air. Just as in World War II, the war had been going on for three years before we began to catch up with an enemy who had been making ready long before he attacked and was able, therefore, to roll out new and faster aircraft much more quickly than we did.

Even then the Germans were using synchronized guns, firing through the propeller blades of their single-seaters, and the first great German fighter pilots had made their appearance, men like Immelman and Boelcke whose names still rate at the top in the annals of combat flying. Immelman was perhaps the first of the great aerobatic fliers, and his monument, the Immelman Turn, still standard equipment in the lexicon of today's fliers, was regarded as no mean stunt in early 1916. Immelman was also the last (and certainly the greatest) of Germany's sportsmen fighters, the sort of person who, if he saw that his adversary was crippled or out of ammunition, would withdraw from battle, wave a hand, and fly away. The practice did not continue, even in World War I. In this war Nazis have introduced the custom of shooting helpless men dangling under parachutes.

Boelcke was another of the sportsmen, perhaps a greater flier even than Immelman, but, like all the other early German air fighters, he looked on Immelman as a god. Perhaps a little anecdote will illustrate the attitude.

An English flier's machine had been badly crippled in combat but the pilot managed to crash-land behind the German lines. His German adversary, following him down, landed beside him and, drawing his revolver, said in perfect English, "You are my prisoner, sir." The British pilot replied, "You are Immelman, so I am not ashamed," to which the German answered, "I am sorry to disappoint you for I am not so great. I am only Boelcke."

It was while we were at St. Omer that I had my first sight of the new aircraft which were beginning to come from the production lines of France and Britain. The first I saw was one of the original-type Nieuport fighters, one of the first of the single-seaters. A little daisy of a ship she looked, with all the daintiness of a Parisienne. A year later she would be as obsolete as last Sunday's roast, but in the spring of 1916 she had an extremely lethal look about her, as if she were the mistress of some nabob of the Quai d'Orsay on her way to shoot her lover. You could call her the originator of the fighter-escort idea and not be far off the mark.

About the same time the first of the Martinsydes appeared from Britain. One of them, I remember, skimmed over the lines at 17,000 feet, while I was at St. Omer, took pictures and returned, not merely without having a shot fired at her but without having been either seen or heard by the enemy. Just about then we youngsters were beginning to talk confidently of Allied air supremacy. As for myself, the sight of these sleek new combat machines brought the determination to become a pilot.

We spoke too soon when we talked about air supremacy. We had forgotten that the Germans were working all out to develop even faster machines and that they had a big jump on us in the beginning. We talked big and perhaps we could be forgiven for it, for we had not yet encountered such machines as the Albatros nor such fighting men as Richthofen and the fellows who flew in his circus.

After four months in France as an observer I had a very lucky break. My pilot and I crash-landed. I injured one of my knees and when the torn cartillages refused to mend, I was shipped back to England for proper attention. As a result, I found opportunity to pull a few strings, talk to a few people I knew, and finally to wangle my way to flying school.

Thinking in terms of the instruction drummed into today's young birdmen before they are allowed to fly at all, and of the tremendous number of hours they spend in the air before qualifying for their wings and, even after that, before they are allowed to assume operational duties, the schooling period of the last war looks like a merry jest. Even the medical examination of that day would draw laughter from the scientific M.O. of World War II. As I remember, after the doctor had listened to your heart and banged your lungs and persuaded you to say "aah" and "ninety-nine," you were put into a swivel chair, spun sharply around, and suddenly invited to spring to attention. If you did not fall flat on your face it was then presumed that you were a healthy individual and fit to fly. You also did things like walking a chalk line with your eyes shut. That was about all there was to it.

I moved along to Ground School where, after three weeks spent in studying the theory of flight and imbibing information about the insides of engines which was plain-and-fancy Greek to all of us, I moved on again, this time to learn to fly.

That was about the 1st of November 1916 and I was assigned to a wallowing old crate of the type disrespectfully known as the

"Rumpty," the actual name of which is the Farman biplane. I did not get along very well while flying dual with my instructor. Sometimes I would be roundly cursed for my ham-handedness as I almost froze to the controls in my anxiety to do well. That would send me to the other extreme and on the next attempt I would be "timid-handed"—and if you go timid with a Rumpty the lady is very likely to fly you into the ground just to get even with you for your lack of attention to her. She was not one of those ladies who liked to be rough-housed, but she did like to be treated with a firm hand.

Then came the day of my first solo.

There is not a pilot above ground who won't tell you that this is the greatest day in any flying man's life. I know what it did to me. For weeks I felt a deep and paternal pity for the millions of people who had never flown alone and never would. I had become a knight in shining armor—to myself.

All the trappings were present for such a great occasion, even to the ambulance parked outside the hangar to bring me back alive, I hoped. As I went out to my machine I was glad to notice that the ambulance engine was running and reflected that back in the first-aid room the doctor already was probably sharpening his carving knife and rubbing his hands in anticipation. I may have felt like a king half an hour later, but right then I had that awful dentist's-anteroom feeling in the pit of my stomach. I climbed in and waved a hand to the mechanics at the chocks. That did not entail much effort. All I had to do was hold the hand up. Its natural shakes in themselves constituted a very rapid wave. But I taxied out and nosed into the wind and ran like mad across the field (if you can imagine a Rumpty doing anything so undignified), staggered into the air, climbing steadily, and kept going in a straight line. Now I felt like a king!

The feeling did not last long, because the realization suddenly began to come through that sooner or later I would have to do a turn, come back in the other direction, turn again and, somehow, get back to *terra firma*. Well, a fellow couldn't keep going straight on forever, so, finally, I did what I thought was a first-class bank but which, I was subsequently informed, was one of the best skids ever performed by a pupil. On I came up the back stretch, managed a somewhat better turn, and there I was, over the airdrome!

Given my choice about then, I'd have stayed up in the air forever. The very thought of making contact between undercarriage and Mother Earth was almost too awful to contemplate. Nevertheless it had to be done. So I shut my eyes and pushed the nose down. Then I opened one eye cautiously to see how things were going and came to the conclusion that I was descending at too steep an angle, so I pulled the nose up a bit. This maneuver I repeated again and again, giving the impression to the watchers below that my machine must be walking down an invisible staircase. Finally I leveled off and executed to perfection everything I had been told to do in order to make a perfect landing. The only thing that was wrong was that I executed it 40 feet above the ground. Fortunately for my career in the Royal Flying Corps I noticed this in time, put the nose down again and made another perfect landing, this time only 8 feet above the grasstops. Milady simply fell the rest of the way, banged her sturdy undercarriage onto the field, and groaned to a stop—whereupon young Bishop stepped down feeling like the monarch of all he had surveyed!

I like to contrast this with what happened to the tyro-fliers of the Second World War, described in a later chapter. In World War II a boy spent four months studying all sorts of intricate subjects in Basic Training and Initial Training School before he ever got into an airplane. I know no more apt illustration of what has happened to military aviation in these two wars. It would be possible to set down all manner of technical comparisons, but there is no simpler way of getting across the idea of the tremendous jump which has taken place in the air than in the contrast between the training of the youngsters who flew in 1915 and those who fly now.

CHAPTER 3

First Blood

I OFTEN wonder how the boys who made such tremendous scores against the enemy in World War II and who quickly gave our side supremacy in the air (once the politicians, the designers, and the manufacturers gave them aircraft capable of meeting the *Luftwaffe* on even terms) can be such patient auditors for elderly gentlemen who are constantly telling them what war is all about and how to fight it, usually by pointing out what a grand job the old-timers did in the other big show. But a great many sound comparisons can be made and in the field of aviation it is by comparing the everyday lives of pilots in World War I with those of the airmen of World War II that we get the most vivid picture of military aviation as it was then and as it is now.

In World War I, you were fortunate if you got three hours of an instructor's time, all told. Once he had sent you off, he was through with you.

It reminds me of the story of how babies come into the world. When they are just ready, they are laid in long trays in Heaven and God, going by, looks them over, stamps each in the tummy, and says, "*You're* done!" "*You're* done!" and "*You're* done!" . . . and that's how we get our belly-buttons. That's just about as much as we saw of our instructors. Like the babies, we soloed—and were on our own in the world.

Take night-flying, for example. When we were training in 1916, we had to pass night tests, for British pilots had just begun to take to the night air to drive the Zeppelins away from Britain.

In the autumn of 1916, with all of fifteen hours' solo to my credit and brand new wings on my chest, I was sent to the mouth of the Thames with one other pilot, whom I regarded as a hoary veteran, as he had the whole of forty hours' solo, to guard the mouth of the Thames against Zeps. Between the two of us we had a 50-mile vital stretch of Britain to protect. Fortunately we never saw a

Zeppelin, as I have always been certain that to run up against one could only have resulted in my going down in an uncontrolled spin, while the dirigible cruised on toward London.

Night-flying in those days in small aircraft was a fearsome business, which I can only compare to being dumped into a strange lake at midnight. We took off between two rows of flares, and soared into the night sky, praying to goodness we would be able to find our airdromes when the time came to return. Our knowledge of navigation was completely elementary. We had a lecture or two in which our instructors tried to drum into our dreary heads some sense of direction and a rudimentary knowledge of the stars in their courses, but it was all Greek to most of us and whenever we flew by night it was strictly by the seat of the pants. I would pick myself a few shadowy landmarks and try to orient myself by them. There was no such thing as voice contact with the ground and there was no Johnny in a control tower telling you what to do and when to do it. Consequently it was always an awesome business to get back to the starting point and, on coming in, to land. You saw plenty of chimney pots and trees which were not there. That was the experience of all the night fighters in the last war, although by the time they had been at it for months they took it as a matter of course, the only alternatives being either to go sick or go mad.

Compare this to our use of the night air now. During the preinvasion weeks of World War II and later, thousand-plane armadas left Fortress England night after night. Ahead flew the Pathfinders to light the targets with parachute flares against the arrival of the big bombers, which then proceeded to demolish Germany's war-industry cities with precision. Night intruders hovered over enemy airdromes waiting for Hitler's night-flying squadrons to come home. The aerial war went on at night with an intensity at least as great as that of the daylight hours. In fact, to the aerial fighter of World War II, the night became a friend, whereas short years ago it was his enemy, an element he had to fight almost as fiercely as his physical foe.

Such are the results of man's rapidly increased, and still increasing, knowledge of his new element, the air. By the time a young man is ready for operational duty at the front the night holds no terror for him. His navigator takes him to the target as skillfully as a sea-captain brings his ship into harbor. He knows all about the winds and the weather, whereas twenty-five years ago we learned about both by the simple process of running into them.

Similarly, to fly by night is taken as casually by the civilian proceeding about his lawful occasions as was the adventure of going to bed in a pullman berth thirty years ago. Today we say as casually, "I'll be home on the midnight plane," as a dozen years ago we told our wives we were catching the evening flier.

As to my assignment as a night-flying Zeppelin hunter, a job which obviously was not my forte, it consisted primarily of sitting on our isolated station, waiting for the telephone to ring to tell us that the Hun was about to visit London. I never liked the job and was extremely happy when I received word at the end of February 1917 that I had been released from the duty of saving Britain and was to be sent to France.

Now I was a single-seater fighter pilot flying the latest type of Nieuport, whose beauty in an earlier version had decided me at St. Omer, a year earlier, to become a pilot. We were, if today's young men will forgive me for saying so, the Spitfire pilots of World War I. But the way we went into action was in no way related to the organized methods by which today's fighters come to grips with the enemy. There were no such things as "scrambles." Sometimes we went off on organized patrols and we were beginning to get the hang of the importance of formation flying, but a great deal of a man's work, particularly if he had shown any proclivity for single-handed combat, was done on his own.

In other words, he pretty much flew according to his own schedule, excepting those occasions when the brass hats called on the telephone to ask for a specific job to be done. From the moment when we took off until we returned, we were out of all touch with home and were completely alone. There was no R.T.—as the British and Canadian Air Forces speak of their ground-to-air communication system—over which to talk to formation mates, or to an Operations Room on the ground. You might have a private code of visual signals with other members of your flight, or with some fellow with whom you flew constantly, but that was all. Nobody could suddenly yell into a mike to warn you of an enemy plane coming at you out of the sun, nor could the ground warn you of an approaching flight of bombers and order you to desist from your current activities and go to meet them. You were your own eyes and your own ears and you were very much by yourself. In fact I doubt if mankind has ever known a lonelier job than that of the single-seater fliers of World War I.

When your airplane was disabled you were done for, unless you were able to get back, complete with machine, to *terra firma.* There were no parachutes, no Mae Wests, and no dinghies in which to sit on the sea until the crash boat came to get you. There was no turning over on your back in a burning aircraft to fall out, pull the ripcord and get away from the mess. You simply sat there and fried.

But the old-timers of World War I pioneered aerial combat. They wrote the fundamental rules, few of which have been discarded, though all have been sharply refined. The pilots of World War I gave the world the science of aerobatics which has not changed much during the intervening years. Perhaps today's aircraft dive at speeds we never dreamed of. If we had been able to develop the dizzy downhill gait of today against the resistances set up by our unstreamlined little ships (which we considered streamlined), the wings would have fallen off. Sometimes they did. It was really *something* when we acquired planes capable of taking us up to 15,000 feet, an altitude at which most of them were pretty soggy on the controls.

Nevertheless the pilots of World War I left a proud heritage, the heritage of the fighting man all down the long corridors of time—the spirit which tells a man to seek out and destroy the enemy, not to wait for the enemy to come to him. If the same spirit had persisted in our leaders during the years between two wars, mankind would never have faced the disasters of Dunkirk or Singapore, of Pearl Harbor and all the other catastrophes brought upon the world by men who refused the issue when it faced them.

You could say that the World War I fliers gave those who fight in the air today the fundamental rules of their technique. The refinements which came along later are the products of aviation science: infinitely better aircraft, engines and armament, and infinitely more scientific selection of men.

It was a madcap crowd who flew the tiny fighters of 1917. By then, of course, we had been given synchronized guns and were by no means as helpless as we had been a year before, but the Germans still enjoyed air superiority on the Western front in 1916 and 1917 and their Albatroses were taking heavy toll, not so much of our single-seaters as of the poor old lumbering BE's that were still doing most of the observation work, and of other two-seater types, always the fighter pilot's "cold meat."

We flew from sun-up to sun-down as often as the weather would let us, and from sun-down to sun-up we sought whatever fun we could find. Often we piled into our squadron cars and drove across country to visit other airdromes and make the night uproarious with song and laughter. We thought nothing of driving 40 or 50 miles to Boulogne for dinner and returning to our airdromes just in time to climb into flying gear and be off over the lines. We made tennis courts behind our hangars, played on them in spotless white flannels and half-way through a set jumped into our cockpits and were off over the lines to fight, still in white flannels. When we nabbed an enemy alive we wined and dined him before he was sent on his way to prison camp, not, as Hollywood would have you believe, to pump the poor unfortunate for information, so much as to observe what we regarded as the rules of chivalry. All sorts of mad incidents happened, for life in the Air Force was always taken externally as a huge joke. There was, for example, the German machine which landed at one of our airdromes one day in May 1917, just after dawn, without being in any way disabled. The pilot was simply lost and the reason for it was not dissociated from the manner in which he and his companion had spent the previous evening. Arising from wassail, they had flown over the lines to demonstrate what manner of men they were, a popular early morning point of view. Thus, when the pilot was challenged at the point of a gun, he stepped out of his cockpit in full mess kit, complete with miniatures of his medals, while from the second cockpit climbed a huge 250-pound German general, also in complete mess gear and jingling with decorations. They had been dining with Richthofen and the general had expressed a desire to have a look behind the British lines before going home to bed. Spotting a British field, they thought they were safely home again. When they discovered they had landed at an enemy airdrome they hastily chewed and swallowed all their personal papers, but when they were searched, the general's pockets debouched four tickets to the theater in Cambrai for the following evening, a show he was destined not to see.

My first patrols in France were certainly not spectacular. I had joined No. 60 Squadron, R. F. C., and on returning from my second flight in one of its precious little Nieuports I crash-landed and wrote off the machine, choosing the very moment when our Wing Commander was present on our field. I was hauled up on the carpet and tried to argue myself clear by saying that a gust of wind had swept around the corner of the hangar and caught me just as I was landing. The Wing Commander thanked me for my explanation and informed me that I would be sent back to the Pilots' Pool at St. Omer, as obviously I was no fellow to be flying such delicate aircraft. Fortunately the senior officer relented when I pleaded for another chance and I was lucky enough on one of my early patrols over the line to score my first decisive victory.

Nobody could have been more surprised than I. My flight was flying along in formation at about 9000 feet, well over Germany, when I spotted three enemy machines out of the corner of an eye, at some distance to the east. A moment later we were involved in a hard-hitting dogfight with a trio of Albatroses. In due course they got around behind us and suddenly we all turned on them and went into action. It was my first taste of a real dogfight and I don't mind admitting I had the shakes as I plowed into it. Imagine my surprise when I let go a burst at my nearest antagonist and saw my tracer bullets hitting the bull's eye! A second later the enemy plane rolled over on its back and began to fall out of control. That was the sort of thing pilots were taught not to take too seriously, for the Germans were building their single-seaters to stand extraordinary strains and stresses, and one of their better fliers' smarter tricks was to go spinning down, apparently out of control, in the hope that the enemy would follow. Then, just as you thought the German was going to spin into the ground, he would snap out, under complete control, to come up smartly under an opponent with guns blazing.

I forgot this aspect of the business, however, in the excitement of thinking I had bagged my first Hun. He spun down about 1000 feet, then regained control. Again I opened fire and this time saw my tracers hitting all around the cockpit. The German's ruse had failed. Down he went again almost vertically, I following. This time he spun right in. I had drawn my first blood and I felt a tremendous sense of exaltation, which quickly passed when I suddenly realized that I had lost touch with my mates and had not the slightest idea where I was, so taken up had I been with attaching myself to that Albatros. I took a hurried look around and decided

I must be deep into enemy territory and turned to fly in the direction which I estimated as being west. Barely had I made my turn, however, when my engine conked. The long dive had filled it with oil and choked it to death. So the finale of my first fight in the air was going to be a forced landing and imprisonment for the rest of the war, if I were so lucky as not to be shot by troops on the ground in the meantime. I glided along trying to think of a way out of the impasse and dolorously picked a place in the shell-pocked terrain under me. Making my last half-turn, I glided in and sat down.

In a moment I was out of the cockpit and, following the hunted animal's instinct to take cover, rolled into a near-by shell hole to catch my breath and survey the scene. Those were anxious moments and they grew more anxious as I saw half a dozen grubby-looking figures creeping out toward my refuge. Nobody will ever know my joy when, as they came closer, their uniforms turned out to be well-mudded khaki and not the German field gray I was expecting to see. I had just wriggled over the lines to our side of the war!

We were convinced that as soon as the German batteries had been told of the forced landing of a hostile aircraft in the forward area they would shell the daylights out of the place. So with the help of my new friends the machine was man-handled to a depression in the ground behind a small hill, where I set to work to try and get the engine going. Not so much as a cough emerged. Finally I packed up for the night and accepted an invitation to spend it with a near-by battery of 18-pounder guns.

From there I tried to establish communication with my squadron to let them know where I was, but no reply came through and I began to think I must have been fired. Next morning, after swallowing an artilleryman's breakfast, I went to work again on the engine. Lo and behold! After a couple of hours of tinkering she ran beautifully because she was no longer choked with oil. I tried to taxi out of my landing field, but disaster came again when a great chunk of mud and rock flew up and split the propeller. Now there was nothing to do but wait for help to come from home. Two days later a repair gang from my own field arrived, dismantled my machine, loaded it into a lorry, and lugged it back to our airdrome.

How different then and now!

CHAPTER 4

The First Great Surge

IN AN earlier chapter we have spoken of the years of World War I as having been a time of tremendous impetus in the development of aviation. One brief phrase, to me, sums up the whole matter: World War I *made* aviation.

There was something tremendous about that period of surge between 1914 and 1918. To people who were not present, or who have only known aviation in its present flashing raiment, what happened then probably looks very dull and slow-poke. On that score there is only this to say: if that tremendous forward movement had not taken place as and when it did under the impact of war, with keen competition between the two opponents for control of the skies, aviation would still be lumbering along far behind the mark it had reached at the beginning of World War II.

In the first place, what happened in the skies of war before her own entry, opened the eyes of America to the possibilities of flight and set her forward-looking people to dreaming about the future. Excepting those who flew in the forces, comparatively few people in the United States, in the field of manufacturing or anywhere else, became even remotely air-minded until after the war. There were good reasons; two and a half years of a war which lasted only slightly more than four passed before the United States became involved, and Uncle Sam was not spending those two and a half years in getting ready to fight as he did in the latter part of 1940 and down to the time of Pearl Harbor. In World War II the United States' aviation industry was of such great assistance to the Allies, and certainly to the countries which comprised the British Commonwealth when we stood alone after Dunkirk, that it would not be overemphasis to say that Britain's friends in the Western Hemisphere kept her alive in the air, in so far as aircraft of the types generally described as bombers are concerned. In World War I the reverse was the case and only the equipment which poured from the factories of Britain and France made it possible for America to fight in the air at all. Not one combat airplane came to the battlefront from the factories of the United States, the sole contribution being airplanes for training, like the Curtiss Jenny of revered memory. The mass-produced Liberty engine, used in quantity in such R.A.F. fighting machines as the DH9, rendered magnificent service, however, and taught British aero-engineers much about quantity production.

If the American people were not very war-like until their country was actually engaged—and so made little preparation in advance—the reason is not difficult to find. After all, having elected a President for a second term on the slogan "He kept us out of war," they were entitled to believe that he would continue to do so—a naïve point of view, admittedly, but, after all, North Americans are naïve people.

Putting an end to speculation, let us look briefly at what was happening in the countries whose people were fighting for their lives against Germany in 1914 and 1915, virtually the same countries which shouldered the burden again in 1939. In these countries, and in the United States and Canada, the first group of airplane builders and fliers had appeared—men like Santos-Dumont in France, the Wrights and others in America—and gave aviation its start. Then came the first military designers. In France they gave us the Nieuport and the Spad. Britain moved through the BE's and RE's to the first single-seaters, such machines as the Sopwith Pup, and its successor, the Camel. Paralleling these came the great SE5, the infinitely maneuverable little beauty whose pilots regarded themselves as the aristocrats of the air. In the realm of the two-seaters one of the greatest gaps in aviation history was bridged between the first observation machines and such grand combat aircraft as the Bristol Fighter and the two magnificent contributions of De Havilland, the DH4 and the DH9.

Much pioneering was being done by our enemies, too, after beginning the war with the patents of such great designers as Holland's Tony Fokker, whom Britain had cold-shouldered. Germany's Albatros was the greatest of all the single-seaters until late in the war. Certainly her Gotha bomber, father of all daylight bombing, gave England a bad time, while in reverse, our Handley-Pages were giving the Germans plenty of trouble in the region behind their lines. Thus practically every form of military aviation as we know it today had its inception during those years. Air fighting, machine-to-machine and man-to-man, began then. Ground strafing was born when intrepid young men in two-by-four single-seaters used to dive on plodding troops and scatter them with bursts of machine-gun fire. Aerial photography became a science during those self-same years. The bombing of strategic targets and the destruction of enemy installations from the air was in the growing-pains stage during the last two years of World War I, and had been experimented with by the Germans, through the medium of lighter-than-air ships as early as 1915. Thus, when we came to World War II, the basic formulas were practically those with which we finished the first war in the air. The advances made had been in the realm of refinements. By the same token, it was during the course of the Second World War that aviation moved forward again into realms of which only a few scientists dreamed when hostilities began in 1939.

The public tendency is to think that the great developments in military aviation of World War II have come in the fields of speed and range. No doubt these have been of vast importance, but they came as natural forward trends. The real developments have come from other quarters.

What has really made possible the tremendously increased efficiency of combat and transport aircraft has been the great outpouring of precision instruments to equip the flying man of World War II. In every bomber which takes to the air on a war-like mission sits a navigator as efficient as, and probably more efficiently equipped than any mariner sailing the high seas. In the same machine you will find a bombardier (in Canada we call them bomb-aimers) outfitted with gear which enables his Fortress or Halifax to lay its eggs in the middle of the enemy's nest, whereas in the first air war our little flying hens used to drop theirs at random all over the barnyard. Our night-fliers used to come home principally by relying on prayer. In World War II their sons returned from operations which had carried them hundreds of miles afield, and neither fog nor storm could prevent them from reaching harbor. Experts in electronics and all manner of other scientific gentry are bringing the flier back alive today. It is in the field of science, therefore, and in the aids which science gives to the aviator, that the greatest advance has been made. It is an advance of greater significance than that which has taken place in the fields of speed or flying range, and it is a species of advance which should cause any man of good will to inquire in deep seriousness: "Where do we go from here?"

People often ask me how I think the pilots of World War II stack up beside their fathers who flew in World War I. How anyone dare try to answer that question I don't know. Is the man who drives the latest product of the assembly line of the modern automobile factory a better chauffeur than his father who drove a Model T? Who knows? The relationship in expertness lies only in the fact that each is driving a contraption with a stationary engine under its bonnet. But from that point forward any resemblance between their activities is purely accidental.

I mentioned in an earlier chapter that in World War I a man might be flying in mortal combat before he had twenty hours' solo in his log book, whereas in World War II nobody would have dreamt of letting a boy so much as thumb his nose at a German until he had at least two hundred hours under his belt. We cannot compare armament or precision equipment, sturdiness or speed of today's machines with the stuff men flew in 1917. But there were combat fliers around in those days who would have been topnotch men under any conditions. In other words, the eye is no keener than it was, no matter how many raw carrots a man may eat. Human courage has reached out to no new heights. If Richthofen had been twenty in 1939 he would still have been Richthofen, with all the bizarre personality of that strange young man and his love for shooting sitting birds. If Canada's Bill Barker had been born in this century instead of the last he would still have had the time of his life chasing Germans around the mountains of Italy. A Rickenbacker would still have been Rickenbacker, a Guynemer would still have been Guynemer. And a Hun is still a Hun, which seems to be one of Nature's Great Unchangeables.

As an aside, concerning Richthofen, I may be forgiven if I add my two cents' worth to a controversial discussion which has been raging for a quarter of a century, as to by whom and by what means the great German ace was finally killed.

Richthofen was shot down in 1918 over a sector held by Australians. When infantrymen reached the scene of the crash behind the Allied lines, they noted that the great German pilot had been brought down by one bullet which had pierced his heart. His machine was unscathed, save for the effects of the crash.

At the time of Richthofen's death a Canadian pilot, Roy Brown, had been in a dogfight with the German and when last seen and heard had been on the Baron's tail and firing at him with his synchronized machine gun. When Richthofen's body was examined it was agreed that the killer's bullet had entered the German from the direction in which shots fired by Brown would have pierced him. Troops on the ground in the immediate vicinity, however, vowed that Richthofen had been killed by a bullet fired by an Australian Intelligence Officer whose name I have never heard.

Well, the chances in favor of Brown having destroyed Richthofen are infinitely greater than are those of the Aussie. If you credit the gentleman from Down-Under, then you do so on the basis of one chance shot fired at a man who was going across the sky at a speed of at least 140 miles an hour hundreds of feet above the marksman's head. In which case the Aussie either set an all-time high in marksmanship, or a new record in miracles. The reader may take his choice.

If you give credit to Brown, on the other hand, the Canadian was in an ideal position to do exactly what he seems to have done. Their speeds were approximately equal, target and marksman were virtually stationary in relation to each other, excepting whatever changes in relative positions may have resulted from aerobatic movements either may have made. Against this, however, must be taken into consideration the fact that Brown was not one of the world's great shots, but was just a first-class hard-working air fighter who did his chores efficiently and came home, as hundreds like him were doing every day.

Yet even this line of thought tends to sway the evidence in Brown's favor. If he had held a reputation for marksmanship, people would have wondered what happened to all the other bullets in the burst he fired. Inasmuch as he was never a great man with a gun, however, no fellow-flier has ever been in the least surprised to know that the rest of the burst failed to get on any part of the target. As far as I am concerned, I believe Roy let go pretty much all over the sky, probably while skidding, and that Richthofen was so unfortunate (from his point of view) as to fly directly into the path of one bullet. That is infinitely more likely to be what happened than that a man on the ground fired one shot from a rifle and performed one of the greatest single feats of the whole war.

If the Aussie claim is valid, it certainly leaves every ack-ack gunner of the future a mark to shoot at for the rest of time. But nobody will ever convince anyone who flew in World War I that Richthofen was shot down by anyone but Roy Brown. Brown was never given official credit for the kill. Had he been in any other air force in the world then or now, he *would* have been given credit and would probably have received at least half a dozen decorations from his own and Allied countries, for to destroy Richthofen could be described as the equivalent of shooting down fifty enemy machines with one bullet. But the British are a conservative crowd and they don't give away credits for knocking down airplanes, or for sinking submarines, as long as any possible vestige of doubt remains. In short, the killer must be in possession of substantiating evidence which would stand up in any court in the world. In the case of a British or Canadian flier bringing down an enemy aircraft, his kill must be checked either by fellow-pilots or by eye-witnesses on the ground. There were eye-witnesses to Brown's feat, plenty of people who saw the dogfight and the crash, but there were also a few people who saw the one shot fired from below. As far as I am concerned, the one chance shot from the rifle of an excited young man, vouched for in good faith by his immediate associates, robbed Roy Brown of official recognition for one of the greatest, if luckiest, shots of the whole war.

The reader may ask: "Why bring such a subject up at this particular juncture; why not let a sleeping dog lie?"

Roy Brown died the other day after a lifetime spent in aviation, both in war and peace; one of the most useful lives aviation has known. Roy spent none of his years looking for credit or trying to live on the results of this one great achievement, for which all his fellow-Canadians certainly gave him credit. He simply came back from the war and, as the Canadian people tackled the job of opening their great North country through the medium of the airplane, jumped into that new field of high adventure and gave his life to it as assiduously as he had given it to combat flying overseas. Since his death, however, the dispute has been renewed and dispatches have reached America from Australia again maintaining that Brown was not entitled to the credit for killing Richthofen. In fact, one gentleman has made so bold as to say that he and he alone deserves recognition. So I am simply saying a word on the subject because Roy Brown was my friend and because I admired him, his way of life, and his outlook. Brown always said that it didn't matter a damn who shot Richthofen, what mattered was that he *was* shot down. That suits me. But I doubt if you will ever find a man who flew with the R.A.F. at that time, and who knows the circumstances, who will not jump up at the drop of an expletive, to fight all over again for Brown.

In any case, the R.A.F. took title to Richthofen's body and buried it with every honor which can be accorded to a great airman. At least they can't take *that* away from us. And that brings me back to Richthofen and to the remark that while aviation has undergone revolutionary changes, the character of men and races remains constant.

Richthofen's fighting methods were typically German. That is not said to belittle the Baron's qualifications, but it is certainly not said in admiration of the German Junker's qualities either. True, Richthofen piled up a tremendous score before Brown finally destroyed him, but he did not pile it up as hundreds of young men who flew for Britain, America, and France acquired their credits. He did not fly with the devil-may-care abandon of a Barker, a Rickenbacker, a Ball, or a McCudden. He flew with a cold calculating skill and his great trick was to withhold from battle himself until his own flying mates had set up the target for him. Then Richthofen would come whisking down out of the sun for the kill, pop off the lame duck, and fly away home with another great victory under his belt! In following this system he not merely kept himself out of harm's way, but sacrificed many fine pilots from his own circus, the lads who did the dirty work before the great man jumped in to polish off the enemy and fly away with the credit. I am not particularly critical of his method, other than as I am critical of the Germanic temperament as such. In so far as I am concerned, Richthofen's system was typically German. Just once, Richthofen was beaten to the draw. Brown caught the German while he was waiting to pounce on an enemy already deeply engaged—another sitting bird. So even the way of his departure was typical of the people who produced the Nazis, just as what Brown did in his David-versus-Goliath act was typically British or North American, or democratically individualistic. It is the fundamental reason why the Germans lose wars.

From all of which you may gather that I do not think highly of the breed who live on the other side of the Rhine, a people with a genius for wrecking the peace of the world and for finishing in second place. I leave to others the entertaining of charitable feelings toward the people of Germany. Let others say that the German people have been bamboozled by Hitler. I say they will always be bamboozled by leaders who offer them another shot at world conquest, just so long as we permit the practice to continue.

CHAPTER 5

Per Ardua Ad Astra

THE thousands of young men who flew in combat in World War I made a tremendous contribution to the world's air-mindedness, and the spectacular quality of their deeds did more than turn the world's attention to the men themselves; it made the world, consciously or otherwise, do its first thinking about aviation as such.

Mention has already been made of the greatest of all German aces, Manfred von Richthofen, and the attempt undertaken to bring to cold type a vignette of his personality and the way he fought, because Richthofen was typically German and Junker. Now I would like to talk about a fellow who flew on our side, the deadliest air fighter of all, a man whose qualities have not even been exceeded in World War II. The point to be made is that the Revolution of the Air has not changed the basic characteristics of the men and nations who fight our aerial wars.

He was a Canadian and his name was Billy Barker. Like so many North Americans who have left their imprint on the pages of combat, he came from a midwest prairie farm and had no experience of war, or aviation, and little of the world itself, when he joined the Canadian forces in 1914 as a private soldier. In this respect at least he bears a marked resemblance to America's young Major Bong. It was 1916 before Barker transferred from the infantry into the old Royal Flying Corps, which he joined, like myself, as an observer, in which role he had more experience than I, for by the time he went back to England from France to learn to fly he had already been wounded and had won the Military Cross.

Billy Barker went back to the war as a pilot early in 1917, this time as chauffeur of a two-seater artillery observation machine. After a tour of operational duty at the front he was sent back to England to be an instructor.

Barker felt completely frustrated by living in a Training Squadron, teaching other youngsters how to fly. He applied to be returned to operational duties, but the application was denied. Whereupon he took a most unmilitary and undisciplined step and decided to make himself such a nuisance to the staff that they would be glad to see the last of him. Day after day he was pulled up on the carpet for low flying over towns, for stunting over headquarters, and for playing the fool generally. Called to account by his superiors he promptly informed them that he intended to misbehave and commit compound fractures of the rules until such time as the brass hats decided to post him back to the front.

So Barker was sent back to France by his irritated superiors, this time to fly a Sopwith Camel, that delicate piece of sudden death with which British pilots wrought so much havoc amongst the Albatroses in the later months of the war.

Barker was the originator of one great trick. That was to lure his enemies into battle as close to the ground as possible, for he had made the discovery that the Camel was infinitely more maneuverable close to the ground than any airplane the Germans possessed.

The first great test of the Barker system came one day at dusk when he was leading his flight home, but was still deep in German-held territory. Suddenly ten planes appeared in the half-light heading east: German Albatroses on their way home. Barker and his friends went in to attack.

Early in the melee the Canadian pilot, while going to the assistance of one of his mates, found himself with a Hun on his own tail. This was his chance to try out the system. Zig-zagging to keep out of range of the German's guns, Barker circled lower and lower, making no attempt to get into shooting position, coaxing the German pilot right up the garden path. He led the enemy almost down to the treetops, then suddenly—and suddenly is altogether too slow a word—went into a tight loop with his small, quick Camel. The slower Albatros could not cope with such activities. In a split second Barker was on the German's tail and with one quick burst destroyed him.

Almost before the first had crashed, a second pounced on Billy. Using the identical tactics he crashed the second German in flames, zoomed away, and made for home in the falling light. Such a master of low fighting did Barker become in the next few weeks and such a madcap devil was he in his sheer youthful exuberance that Headquarters hit on a brainy idea and formed a squadron of youngsters who were then trained to the Barker system and shipped to Italy to fight the Austrians and Germans in the mountain passes.

In Italy Barker's bunch ran wild. They blew Austrian captive balloons, hitherto unmolested, out of the sky far behind the lines. They strafed enemy airdromes at grasstop height, pouring inflammable bullets into the open doors of hangars to set them aflame. They played particular and general hell with the easy-going Austrians.

The enemy, including German reinforcements sent to the Italian front to deal with this mad Canadian and his lunatic youngsters, tried bombing Barker's airdrome with more than thirty German Gothas and on the first try lost almost half their force when Barker and his boys soared up into battle. Barker had now developed a new brand of attack much used in World War II. It is called the head-on system and it takes plenty of guts to be properly executed and get your man, because you must fly at him on his level, straight down his path toward him, and keep going until somebody weakens. I cannot remember ever having met a German who did not duck first. They certainly used to duck when they saw Barker coming.

That was Billy's way of dealing with the Gotha bombers, and on his first encounter he took two out of three by this device. That, in my opinion, must have been one of the great shows of the war. The three Germans were flying in line astern and Barker flew head-on to meet them. He nabbed the first when they were almost bow to bow, ducked under the second, came up head-on into the third, knocked it out of formation, turned on it, and plunged the big Gotha to earth a flaming wreck.

But it was in low flying where he always excelled. Most pilots preferred the more formal method of getting up high, between the enemy and the sun, and pouncing on him from that vantage point. Barker wanted them down near the ground and to find them near the ground meant he practically had to visit their airdrome and lie in wait. His superiors considered him completely mad, but the system worked and soon Billy was knocking enemy aircraft down like flies. Decorations came his way one after the other. The D.S.O. was soon added to the M.C., won as an observer. Then came a bar to his D.S.O. and a bar to his Military Cross. Early in May 1918 the Italians decorated him and Barker subsequently confided in me that, while it was nice to be honored by one's Allies, it was *not* nice to be kissed on both cheeks by a man with a beard.

Perhaps one of the funniest stories about this terrific fighting man is what his friends call the Spy Story.

The practice had come into vogue of flying Allied spies across the enemy lines and dropping them by parachute to do their jobs. At that time, of course, very few people knew much about chutes and extremely few thought highly of dangling under the silk to descend to the ground in the middle of the night. Consequently, it was often the case that a spy would set off in the rear cockpit of an aircraft to be dropped at an appointed place by the pilot, but prior to arrival would achieve understandable frigidity of the feet and decide not to make the jump. To meet this problem Barker, who had had a couple of experiences with mind-changing spies, devised his own system, which was simply to equip the passenger seat with a trapdoor arrangement operated by a lever from the pilot's cockpit, the passenger being totally unaware of the arrangement. Then Barker would fly off with his spy for delivery behind the Austrian lines, keeping the nervous gentleman comforted with reassuring noises as they flew along. When the appointed destination was reached Billy simply sprang the trap. The spy fell out through the floor and died a thousand deaths while he waited for his parachute to open. Inasmuch as each passenger traveled on a one-way ticket, it was not difficult to keep the system secret from prospective riders. Thus for some time Billy operated a spy delivery service which won him high repute with the Intelligence staff.

The greatest Barker story of all relates to three famed Austrian pilots with whom Billy and his teammates sought combat but who had consistently ducked whenever Barker and his Camels appeared on the scene. They were looking for sitting birds, nice quiet artillery observing two-seaters, not maniacs who seemed to be able to do anything they liked with their midget fighting machines.

So Barker had thousands of leaflets printed, and dropped them behind the Austrian lines. The leaflets carried the following challenge:

> Major W. G. Barker, D.S.O., M.C., and the Officers under his command present their compliments to
>
> Captain Brumowsky,
> Rither von Fiala,
> Captain Havratil,

and the pilots under their command and request the pleasure and honour of meeting in the air. In order to save Captain Brumowsky, Rither von Fiala and Captain Havratil and the Gentlemen of their party the inconvenience of searching for them, Major Barker and his Officers will bomb Godega Aerodrome at 10:00 A.M. daily, weather permitting, for the ensuing fortnight.

Barker and his young men carried out their schedule to the letter and the moment. They bombed Godega daily through the fortnight. Once or twice the enemy appeared. But they were face-saving appearances and Barker, as always, came out on top by a lopsided score.

Billy left Italy in the summer of 1918 and returned to Britain to pursue a new course in air-fighting tactics—a young man off to school to learn from the book he had practically written. As always he rebelled against the discipline and red tape of the war behind the lines. This time he evolved a new excuse to get back into combat and asked to be allowed a few weeks at the front in France before taking the course, to acquaint himself with new German tactics. There, on October 27, 1918, only two weeks before the Armistice, and on the flight which was supposed to take him back to Britain, he put on a show which stands as the greatest in the annals of World War I, and one which it would be hard to tie in the later to-do.

The official account states that Barker, having packed his kit and seen it shipped to England, climbed into the Sopwith Snipe he was to fly back, but couldn't resist taking one more look at the lines. He decided to do a little wandering and to have one last look at the war he was on the point of leaving. Instead of turning toward the Channel he swung off over the lines. In a few moments he saw a German machine at 22,000 feet and attacked. The German observer fired so accurately that the Canadian's own machine was badly hit. As Barker's journey was to have been routine and peaceful, the telescopic sight had been stripped off his guns before taking off, so Bill was equipped with ordinary peep-sights, nothing else. Twice he attacked the German before he was able to kill the observer. Then he closed in to short range and shot the pilot and airplane down. The enemy machine broke apart in the air and fell in a rain of small pieces. At this juncture a Fokker pounced on Billy, catching him by surprise, putting an explosive bullet into his right thigh and shattering it. That would have been enough to cause any ordinary fighting man to get out of there, but not Bill Barker. Billy was going to get even. He stayed with his German, finally brought him into the peep-sight for a split second, and sent him reeling down in flames.

Still Billy had not enough, although by then he was fighting to retain consciousness. He must have passed out because, as he told me afterwards, he suddenly found himself in the midst of a crowd of enemy machines, the number of which was estimated by people on the ground as being at least sixty, without having the slightest idea how he got there.

Germans jumped him from every corner of the sky. His machine was hit repeatedly and he was severely wounded again, this time in the left thigh. He fainted from loss of blood and fell thousands of feet out of control with the whole German circus after him. The rush of air in his wild dive brought him back to life and suddenly he turned on his enemies like a mad dog. By then any hope of survival must have gone from his mind. He was simply going to wreak all the havoc possible before the enemy fliers polished him off. He charged head-on at an enemy machine, thinking to collide with it and take at least one more German with him where he was sure he was going.

But, as always, his bullets were right on the target. Before the collision could occur the German burst into flames and fell out of battle—and Barker had picked up an explosive bullet in his left elbow. To tally the score at this juncture, Barker was now sitting in his cockpit, with one thigh shattered, the other severely wounded, and his left arm limp and useless. He fainted again, and again fell out of control. Again he recovered and again swooped up into the melee. This time he fought the Germans all the way down the long hill almost to the ground and in the course of the battle shot down two more. By then he was close to the ground and still under attack from many German machines. A burst of explosive bullets perforated the gasoline tank under his seat, but by miraculous good luck—and there were no self-sealing gas tanks then—the machine did not take fire. Barely conscious, Barker switched to his auxiliary tank and kept the little Clerget rotary engine spinning. He fainted again and almost spun in, recovering consciousness and pulling out just in time. With the machine almost out of control he put its nose down and headed west, not knowing where he was, and piled his machine into a maze of barbed wire immediately behind the

British lines. Five German aircraft had gone down in that tremendous melee between one man and God knows how many antagonists, a man who was supposed to be quietly flying across the Channel to Britain to take a course in air fighting! They gave Billy the V.C. for that one.

His wounds mended and soon after the end of the war he returned to Canada, where he and I were happy partners in one of the first and most amusing commercial aviation enterprises ever undertaken by foolish young men. The irony of life caught up with Billy Barker soon afterwards. He died by stalling and spinning into the ground just after taking off from Ottawa in one of the first Fairchild machines. So passed a man who, in my book, stands as the greatest air fighter the world has ever known.

Perhaps it is foolish and dull for an old-timer to talk about the old days and the old-time fliers. The business of reminiscence could go on forever with tales of Ball, McCudden, Guynemer, René Fonck, the Lafayette Escadrille and Uncle Sam's own Eddie Rickenbacker. I have purposely taken Barker for comparison with Germany's great Richthofen to give the reader a picture of each man's temper and temperament, of each man's skill and each man's methods. The one, Richthofen, was a cool calculating precision machine, typically German. The other was a highly developed individualist who not only asked no man to go where he would not go himself, but who always led his men into battle and was first into the thick of the fray—and last man out.

There you have a fair comparison between the German temperament and that of young men bred in the individualistic atmosphere of the democracies. Fundamentally it is because of this variant in racial temperaments that Germany loses wars and our side wins them. We start with empty hands, but in the last act, once we have the equipment, the spirit of the American or Britisher, Canuck, Australian, or Russian (and don't think the Russians aren't rugged individualists!) comes through to defeat the German machine-like, calculating precisionists. Aviation has revolutionized our world—but the character of man remains unchanged.

From what has been said the reader may have been able to draw a picture not merely of combat flight as it was in World War I, but of the tremendous strides made by aviation, from blueprint to battle, during those years. We began World War I with a handful of old box kites which could barely struggle into the air, and had a top speed of something like 60 miles an hour. That was not the fault of the few men who were the first aircraft designers (a title of dignity which the world had not even conferred on such people at that time). They had no money excepting what they could pry loose from their immediate friends and their own bank accounts. They had nothing but their faith. That was the sum total of the working capital of aviation prior to World War I. Then war established the value of aircraft as a weapon and the full power of governments was unleashed, with the result that in every bracket, from engines to armament to streamlining, the quality of aircraft moved forward by leaps and bounds. At the end of World War I those who survived were flying tiny single-seaters capable of rising to heights of 15,000 or 20,000 feet, ships which could fly level at that height at speeds of 130 or 140 miles an hour, the controls of which were feather-light, and the aircraft themselves capable of any form of aerobatics known to this day. If World War I had not happened, we should still be many many years behind our present development in the air.

CHAPTER 6

Farewell to Arms

DURING those final hard-hitting weeks of the summer of 1918 the war in the skies raged with unabated fury. The German infantry was cracking, collapsing, at times almost running away. Day by day attacking American, British, French, Anzac, and Canadian forces stormed the Hun before he could consolidate new positions after his latest retreat. In a series of hammer blows, delivered with machine-gun frequency from the sand dunes of Flanders to the Swiss border, the Allied armies pounded and smashed the Germans, who by this time were showing little stomach for the fight.

Upstairs, the Allies had gained definite superiority over the enemy for the first time—after almost four and a half years. Many a German fought back with the courage and abandon of men who know their side is going down to defeat and who throw themselves into the last desperate battle determined to make the enemy pay the highest possible price for victory. But many another refused the challenge. During those last tremendous weeks young men from all over the free world flew the skies of Europe and literally beat the German air force into the ground. They flew along the treetops with the infantry, strafing German positions, breaking up their formations, and literally destroying troops and supply trains attempting to move forward to reinforce the front. No matter where the eye looked over the field of death across which the Allied infantry moved forward to victory, shot-down German aircraft littered the ground, with only here and there one of ours. The first war in the air, then, ended in brilliant and total victory for Allied aviation.

When the end came all of us were gripped by a sense of living in a state of animated suspense, bordering on frustration. What were we going to do next? To what kind of world were we soon to return? Would we be able to find jobs? Would we find the same spirit accorded us by the civilian population which they had shown when we left to fight for freedom? Were we capable, we who had known no other life but warfare for almost five years, of adjusting ourselves to the comparative dullness of peace, accompanied by the necessity to get out and earn a living?

Such questions were in every man's mind once the high celebration of Armistice was behind us. The road ahead looked even more frightening than the daily chores of warfare. In combat you know the score. It is you or the other fellow, and you meet him on those extremely simple terms. But peace is something else. Peace is an indefinite fight for survival. It has about it, like war, an every-man-for-himself quality which sometimes appears to the ex-fighting man to be even more merciless than war. War at least breeds comradeship, whereas in peace a man must be prepared to fight on the basis of dog-eat-dog. That is what the fighting man of 1914–1918 was soon to discover.

In the main he came back to a homeland where people had no conception of what he had been through, no knowledge of the adjustments he had to make in order to become a good citizen, no idea of the jittery unrest in his mind, a condition from which many of the participants of World War I never recovered.

The end of the war saw thousands of expert aviators dispersed to the four corners of Christendom. They were aviators no longer. Now they were merely civilians looking for jobs. Probably in the minds of nine out of ten was the hope that somehow, somewhere, a job could be found which would keep them in contact with flying.

There were three friends of mine, for instance, who had flown at the front and who, like so many of us, could not bear the idea of forsaking aviation for the rest of their lives. They called upon a Canadian Cabinet Minister, telling him that they wanted to establish a triangular air service between the cities of Montreal, Ottawa, and Toronto. Some old Curtiss Jennies were available and the young men wanted the Canadian Government to give them a contract to carry the mails.

The Member of the Cabinet on whom they called smiled at them benignly, advising the young men to put such madcap thoughts out of their minds, look for respectable jobs, marry their sweethearts, and become solid citizens.

"While aviation has been of tremendous value to us in war," the Minister said, "there is no place for it in a world at peace. It has no commercial possibilities and it can never compete with the established modes of transportation."

Those words were said in the spring of 1919. Today the same sort of people are saying that as soon as this war is over we must scrap the world airways we have created in our hour of emergency because we shall have no way of using them economically. Such people smile cynically when anybody talks about flying to Europe for a holiday, or of skimming across the roof of the world to spend a few days in the Soviet Union, or about taking a month off to see what China and her people look like. Such people are today's counterpart of those who in 1919 frustrated the legitimate hopes of the World War I fliers.

A few could remain in the Service. But as yet no one saw the commercial possibilities which before many years were to become the foundation stone of world aviation. The public in every country was entirely without knowledge of aviation itself. People looked on flight as a war stunt. Few dreamed that this newest of all modes of transportation had any other possibilities. Those who were to occupy roles of air leadership a few years later had not yet found the capital with which to experiment. In other words, aviation was ready for development and exploitation, but the public was not ready to assist.

Nobody believed, barring the occasional dreamer in laboratories or drafting rooms, that men soon would fly the oceans. Nobody dreamed of transcontinental sleeper planes, of magnificent airports and terminal facilities as palatial as any modern railway station. A few intrepid souls, determined to continue to fly, picked up old Jennies and suchlike obsolete machines and barnstormed around the county fairs, joyriding the gullible and the courageous at five or ten dollars a ride.

Up in Canada Billy Barker and I decided to become the pioneers of commercial flight soon after we returned home. Although we couldn't make a dollar, we had a lot of fun. We acquired a couple of old flying boats, because Canada is full of lakes, every one of which was a free airdrome or an emergency landing field, and we advertised that we were ready and willing with our "many" aircraft to take on just as much business as our countrymen would like to throw our way.

Our first flight was made from Toronto to Muskoka with Barker and myself as pilots and my wife as passenger. Far more fuss was made about this tremendous adventure than would be made today about a flight from Moscow to New York. The highlight of our progress on this death-defying journey, a matter of not more than 100 miles, was that all along the route, as we passed overhead, railway station agents flashed over their telegraph wires the news that the Bishop-Barker flying boat had passed overhead at such and such a time. Presumably it was expected that we would fall to earth without warning, somewhere between two reporting points. But we landed intact at Muskoka and were acclaimed as heroes.

That was the status of aviation in North America in 1919 and 1920. You could no more have gone to a serious banker and have taken money away from him for a commercial flying venture than you could persuade him today to invest in an Axis victory. Such capital as Barker and I had consisted of our own resources plus all that we could coax out of the pockets of friends—the latter moneys probably regarded as charitable donations made to a couple of pleasant lunatics who sooner or later would break their fool necks and so rid their friends of further expense.

In the meantime, however, a few wise men were studying the possibilities of flight. Some were designers—scientific fellows. And scientists seldom have money. Some were forward-looking businessmen in whom the spirit of adventure lived and who possessed the great North American instinct for knowing that, as the world is a constantly changing place, the bright fellow is the one who can see and prepare for tomorrow today.

Through such men as these, civil aviation got its start throughout the world, adapting itself in each country, or on each continent, to the circumstances and needs of the community. In Europe, where intercity distances are short and where the public was perhaps more air-minded than on our continent because it had witnessed the intensive flight of the war years, intercountry passenger services became the bedrock of aviation. Intercity services in the United States were not popular for several years, partly because the aircraft in use were by no means palatial, partly because of lack of regulation and safety, and because, too, the general public clung tenaciously to the belief that a sensible man always keeps one foot on the ground. Canada, in the meantime, pioneered what, in the early days of commercial flight, was without question the most useful purpose for which aircraft could be used—the opening of remote districts for the purposes of peace. In this case the immediate result was the development of valuable mining properties through carrying men, supplies, and machinery over hitherto impenetrable hinterland.

And while the peacetime possibilities of aviation were being brought home to the Western Democracies, Germany was hard at work, making ready for the second war in the air.

PART III

The Years of Growing Pains

CHAPTER 1

The Death of One-Foot-on-the-Ground

ALTHOUGH a great majority of those who had flown in World War I found themselves grounded by the Armistice and returned to routine civilian life on the ground, the handful of war fliers to whom aircraft were still available did not long remain inactive. The first great adventure they tackled, as was to be expected, was the conquest of the Atlantic. Before the first year of peace had passed the first ocean crossings had been made by air.

The first attempt was that of Harry Hawker who essayed the jump from Newfoundland to Ireland. Hawker came to grief, however, some hundreds of miles short of the coast, but was fortunate enough to be fished out of the sea by a passing ship.

The next attempt was successful. It was made by Captain John Alcock and Lieutenant A. Whitten Brown, with Harbour Grace, Newfoundland, as its starting point and Clifden in Galway, Ireland, as its eastern terminus. Great excitement attended the departure of these flights from Newfoundland. The press of the world gathered en masse in St. John's, Newfoundland, to see the Atlantic fliers take off and great speculation ensued both in America and Europe as to the possibilities of success. As a general estimate, the world conceded the gentlemen little chance. To a cynical but air-ignorant world they were "madmen," just as Blériot and *his* contemporaries had been looked upon as mad at the time of the first Channel crossings. So goes the story of all pioneering ventures.

Alcock and Brown took off from Harbour Grace on the 14th of June 1919, in a Vickers Vimy biplane, and disappeared into the gray skies of the Grand Banks. Fifteen hours and fifty-seven minutes later, around the corner into the next day, the two fliers landed in Ireland. The first of the great oceans had been spanned by air! But could it have been said that the Anglo-Saxon world foresaw in this brave show the birth of regular intercontinental and global flight? Such possibilities did not appear to cross the minds of the newspapermen or their readers. Like Blériot's stunt, to the general public in the democracies it was an act of high adventure, nothing else.

In all conscience it *was* high adventure, for not only were the machines of the day not constructed to fly such distances, but they could only attempt such flights by carrying dangerous overloads of fuel. That made even the take-off an extremely ticklish business. The plane would roll on and on and on along the ground until it seemed she would never be airborne and must crash into a tree or a fence at the end of the airdrome. It was adventure all right—high and low. But it was something else as well. It was pioneering in the ultimate sense of the term. But for the madmen who blazed the trails, aviation would have waited long years to clear the way between the continents.

In the same year United States Navy fliers tackled the Atlantic in more conservative fashion, two flying boats taking off from the American side (one of which, NC3, subsequently turned back), NC4 making the crossing in easy stages via Bermuda and the Azores.

So were the first Atlantic flights made. The man wise in the ways of geography knew then that aviation soon would become a factor to be reckoned with in visualizing the future. Such flights gave the lie direct to those "experts" in and out of government who had been insisting that, while aviation had played an important role in war, it had nothing to commend it as man's servant—or man's master—in time of peace. Few government authorities in the Western Hemisphere, in fact, could be impressed by the need for proper controls and regulations to govern even domestic flight.

Not for some years was commercial aviation to be established on an organized footing to compete with other means of transportation in the Americas. Meanwhile serious men attempted, but for years with indifferent success, to prevail on governments to write rules to regulate the new and startling method of human movement. The politicians persistently avoided the issue for years, dismayed, perhaps, by the lack of precedent.

The fact that in the early 1920's aviation failed to win public confidence in the United States was in considerable degree the fault of the government in Washington, first, because it sold off many obsolete planes deemed unsafe for Army or Navy use, with only the mildest warning to purchasers that these aircraft required complete overhauls before being taken into the air; secondly, because, in the free and easy atmosphere of the early postwar years, anybody who had the price of an airplane could buy one and try to fly it. Many fatal accidents followed, for exactly the same reasons that killings would occur if we were to give loaded revolvers to four-year-olds. They served to give the impression that flight is an extremely risky business, which it was under the circumstances.

Such passenger travel as was carried on in those years was mainly conducted by gypsy pilots, the old-time "barnstormers." Airports were few and far between and aids to flight and navigation were virtually non-existent. What was true of the United States was equally true of Canada and the rest of the Americas. In the European countries, and notably Britain, however, a more responsible approach was taken. Not only were the commercial possibilities of flight foreseen, but the use of far-flung airways as links of an Empire chain of communications was visualized as soon as hostilities closed and plans were laid to establish them.

In the strictly commercial realm, the first flight from London to Paris took place on July 15, 1919, and in August of that year regular service was inaugurated between the two capitals by Handley Page. Institution of service between London and Brussels came on September 21 and on the 10th of November airmail was flown between London and Paris, at a rate of 2/6, or approximately sixty cents, an ounce.

Meanwhile the Empire airway chain was in process of birth. Leaving England on November 12 in a Vickers Vimy, Captain Ross Smith and Lieutenant Keith Smith flew to Australia in easy point-to-point stages and reached the land of the Southern Cross on December 10. Between the 4th of February and the 20th of March 1920, Colonel Pierre van Ryneveldt and Captain Quintin Brand made the first England-to-Capetown flight, by way of Cairo. Like Alcock and Brown, and the two Smiths, they flew a Vickers Vimy. Again the world was being contracted in size, as it had been successively by the voyages of Columbus, the *Mayflower*, and the first steamships.

In Europe the extension of passenger and mail services continued and on July 5, 1920, Handley Page established the first London-to-Amsterdam service. In the same month the cost of sending a letter by air from London to Paris was reduced from half a crown to two-pence an ounce. Airmail between London and Brussels was inaugurated in the same month and in August the British Post Office issued its first airmail labels.

The next four years witnessed many great pioneering flights.

Soon the binding together of the Empire and the mother country by a network of air routes would be an accomplished fact. That was the imperial mind of Britain looking aloft and visualizing a world-wide Empire, the members of which would become air-neighbors instead of widely separated sea-associates.

In October 1921 the Royal Air Force provided machines for an airmail service between Cairo and Baghdad. Other services were inaugurated between Britain and the Continent in 1922 and 1923, notably between London and Berlin, and London and Cologne. By the spring of 1924 the London-to-Paris and London-to-Cologne services were operating daily and by summer, service between London and Switzerland, via Paris, was in operation.

Nor was exploration of the all-red route (so called because on most British maps countries in the British Empire are shown in red) permitted to lapse. That year Allan Cobham, one of Britain's famed world aviation pioneers, made the first of many survey flights on the Government's behalf, laying out the route from London to Rangoon. The following year Cobham surveyed the Capetown route and in 1926 established the best line of flight between England and Australia, using a DH50 on floats. The Empire aviation network was taking shape.

In 1924 Britain also took the most important of all her policy steps, one destined to lead British aviation into channels far different from those in which it has developed in the Americas. That was the creation of Imperial Airways as the "chosen instrument" to develop British world air transport as a going concern throughout the world. Imperial absorbed as its components the principal British private operators of the day, Handley Page, Daimler Airways, British Marine Air Navigation, and the Instone Air Line. By 1926 the subsidized "chosen instrument" was in full operation and was flying such giants of the air, as they seemed at the time, as the *City of Baghdad,* first of the three-engined monsters to ply the Far East. *Baghdad* was intended to operate from Egypt through Iraq to India, but difficulties with the Government of Iran on matters of air sovereignty caused suspension of the service for some time. A weekly Cairo-Basra service was started during the next year, however, and by 1929 Britain and India were connected by a weekly mixed air and rail service which greatly reduced the time of passage between the mother country and its great Eastern possession.

Development continued. In 1931 Imperial reached deep into Central Africa with a weekly mail and passenger service which connected London with Mwanza, below the equator in Tanganyika. The England-to-India route was extended to Australia in co-operation with Australian interests, and the Hannibal and Heracles biplane types, the first great four-engined airliners which were to be the work-horses of Britain's far-flung air routes for a decade to come, made their appearance. The Hannibals carried eighteen passengers and developed a maximum speed of 120 miles an hour. They were used on the long-distance runs, while planes of the Heracles class, of similar design but with modifications of construction, were used on the short runs, as between London and Paris. They carried thirty-eight passengers and developed a speed of 127 miles an hour.

In conjunction with South Africa Airways the England-Tanganyika service was extended to Capetown in 1932 and the British had completed a network of Empire airlines operating to virtually every corner of their dominions and possessions, excepting those in the Americas.

The Atlantic was still the hard nut to crack; in fact not until April 1928 was that ocean spanned non-stop from east to west by a heavier-than-air machine. That was the flight of the German Baron von Huenefeld, Pilots Koehl and Fitzmaurice, and the events accompanying it may be regarded as typical of the "stunt" viewpoint of North Americans to the conquering of the world's oceans, an approach far different to that of the British and of Europeans generally.

Many attempts to perform the east-west crossing had been made. All had ended in disaster. For weeks search parties had explored the wilderness country of northeastern Canada, running down rumors concerning the possible whereabouts of the two great French aces, Nungesser and Coli. Leslie Hamilton and the Princess Lowenstein had disappeared somewhere over the North Atlantic. Britain's Hinchcliffe had failed to make the grade. Others, too, had given their lives in the attempt to span the ocean east-west. Finally two Germans and an Irishman made it, although they failed by a matter of approximately a mile to reach the American mainland. The press of the continent promptly went wild, primarily because of the difficulties involved in establishing touch with three airmen marooned on a tiny island in the icebound Strait of Belle Isle.

All manner of rescue parties were organized. First to depart was an old Fairchild flown by the famed Canadian bush-pilot, Duke

Schiller, who lost his life in a crash at Bermuda during World War II, while flying as a captain for the R.A.F. Transport Command. Close on his tail went a second Fairchild, piloted by Romeo Vachon, French-Canadian bush-aviator of almost equal repute. From New York all manner of airplanes tried to buck the appalling early spring weather of the Gulf of St. Lawrence country, carrying newsreel photographers, still-cameramen, special writers, and all manner of publicists. They were downed by weather all over the northeastern states and the Province of Quebec. The New York *World* and North America Newspaper Alliance sent the great Bernt Balchen and Floyd Bennett as co-pilots of a tri-motored Ford to bring out the beleaguered aviators. Tragedy descended on the base camp at Lac Ste. Agnes, near the well-known Canadian summer resort of Murray Bay, when Bennett contracted pneumonia and was flown to a hospital in Quebec, where he died. Meanwhile Charles Lindbergh hastened north by air from New York, carrying pneumonia serum with which it was hoped to save Bennett's life and, if memory serves, brought the same kind which was already available in quantity and being used on the patient in the Canadian hospital.

Days passed while the "rescuers" attempted to reach Greenley Island and while the battle for exclusive news stories raged. The Canadian writer, my own good friend, Leslie Roberts, was the first to establish touch and signed Baron Huenefeld to an exclusive contract with the Hearst press. Fitzmaurice had signed on a dotted line with the *New York Times* before the take-off from Ireland, but the *Times* failed to get a reporter to Greenley Island and, as the story goes, Roberts ghosted for the Baron, for Fitzmaurice, and even for their rescue pilot, Schiller, during a ten-day stretch while "rescuers" and "rescuees" were attempting to make their way in Schiller's plane along the storm-tossed coast of the Gulf of St. Lawrence, back to Lac Ste. Agnes.

The story is set down for the purpose of establishing the attitude of the American press and public to aerial pioneering in those strange days. Few responsible daily newspapers on this continent ever reflected seriously on the implications of such flights. All attempts to span the Atlantic, successful or disastrous, were viewed as adventurous stunts, not as the precursors of scheduled and organized flight back and forth across the gray wastes of the ocean. With such a viewpoint advanced almost unanimously by the American press, it was in no way surprising if the public failed to grasp the tremendous events taking shape so rapidly before their eyes and above their heads.

The beginnings of air transport in the United States were not auspicious. The truth is that long-distance air transportation had its real beginnings in and from Europe and, in so far as intercontinental flight was concerned, between Britain and India, South Africa and Australia. More than any other factor, lack of regulation held back the development of air transportation in the United States and not until the Air Commerce Act of 1926 became law was any serious attempt made to recognize the importance of even domestic commercial flight. During the early years the Army was the core of aerial development in the United States. Service fliers mapped and laid out routes, and published navigation charts. Little by little a demand was created for transport service in populated areas, and the Army cheerfully turned its knowledge over to private operators. Until 1926, however, air transportation in the United States, as in Canada and in fact throughout the Western Hemisphere, was a hit and miss business.

More than anything else the natural affinity between the Post Office and the airplane gave aviation its start in America. As far back as 1911 the United States Post Office had experimented in carrying mail by air from Nassau to Long Island, and in 1916 a small token appropriation for the flying of mails was made. In 1918 airmail service was opened between New York and Washington by the War Department, which provided planes and personnel. Later that year the Post Office itself took over the operation with its own equipment. In 1918 a New York-Chicago airmail was inaugurated and in 1920 the service was extended from Chicago to San Francisco.

During 1920 the Government established a chain of radio stations at airports across the United States and these, coupled with increased care in the inspection and operation of aircraft, greatly reduced the hazards with which the mails had originally been flown. It is interesting to note that for a period of fourteen months not one fatal accident occurred in the United States airmail services, a record largely responsible for the inauguration of night-flying over a portion of the coast-to-coast run. A considerable time passed in experimentation and in the equipping of planes and airports for night-flying. In 1923 a lighted airway was opened between Chicago and Cheyenne, Wyoming. Test flights made over this route were completely successful and on July 1, 1924, a regular night service to the West was begun. Thus in the United States the first serious development of utilitarian transportation was sponsored by the Government itself, through the carrying of mails, and it was above all else the excellent record established by the day and night mail fliers which first focused the attention of the American people on the air as a means of safe and rapid human transportation. The American public, however, were by no means as air-minded as were Europeans. They would not achieve that state until luxurious planes and amenities were made available by airline operators.

The Air Commerce Act of 1926 charged the Department of Commerce at Washington with the responsibility of fostering air transportation, of developing and establishing safeguards for its movement, and encouraging the building of airports and the opening of airlines. The Post Office Department then turned over to the Secretary of Commerce the various routes operating under its jurisdiction. The weather bureau of the Department of Agriculture began to supply fliers with reports. Other facilities were introduced. Uncle Sam had been slower to start than had Britain and various European nations, notably France, Holland and Germany, but once the United States jumped in with both feet, the American people moved forward with rapid strides, as is their genius. It must be noted, however, that they thought in terms almost completely domestic, whereas the British and other Europeans thought internationally and globally even then.

Lindbergh's flight from New York to Paris in 1927 perhaps did more than any other single event to stir the emotions of the American nation and awaken the interest of its people in flying. Certainly it was one of the most dramatic, perhaps the most dramatic, of all the great pioneering flights, undertaken and successfully carried out by an unknown young man without backing, flying an airplane not even properly equipped for its task. While the dignified and well-backed Admiral Byrd, with Paris as his announced destination, was still in the make-ready stage and holding front-page spotlight in the nation's press, the unknown Lindbergh and his *Spirit of St. Louis* whisked into New York from the Middle West and, after a brief pause, were off over the ocean, with that don't-give-a-damn bravado so appealing to the American love of the romantic. It was a clean-cut flight, executed with precision and, unlike so many other pioneer flights, it ended at its announced destination, Le Bourget Field in Paris.

Much criticism has been leveled at Charles Lindbergh since that day, but no one can take away the credit for one of the outstanding pioneer flights in all aviation history. Probably it would have been better for the young man and the record if he had stuck to aviation and not taken upon himself the role of soothsayer in the realm of human affairs and world politics, in which he has displayed an outlook which might almost be called pseudo-fascist. But that, after all, is Lindbergh's business—not mine.

It has often been said that the Lindbergh flight was the first event in American aviation which really stimulated financial interests to believe in the commercial possibilities of flight. Certainly in the days which followed 1927 a rapid growth of airlines took place and the air industry, both in the manufacturing and transportation fields, took on a new and infinitely more responsible aspect. Transportation became more closely associated with manufacturing, and money in important quantities began for the first time to be available to those engaged in the industry. By 1930 the United States was moving forward to a point at which it could be said to parallel in domestic development the continental traffic which existed in Europe. The European operators, notably the British, continued to lead the way for some years to come in intercontinental flight, however, owing primarily to the fact that routes could be established which enjoyed access to intermediate landing points between Europe and distant termini, whereas the distances to be traveled on leaving the mainland of North America, east or west, before safe sanctuary may be found, are much greater. It must also be remembered that if American aviation expanded almost entirely internally during those years, that was the spirit of the American people at that time. The rest of the world was none too popular with people living between Portland, Maine, and Portland, Oregon, at that time—the days of splendid isolation.

So ended the first postwar decade. It was largely a period of experimentation, during which great risks were run. It was also a period of primary education in the possibilities of air transportation, in so far as the potential customer, the public, was concerned. By the end of the 1920's, however, the number of people who were determined always to keep one foot on the ground had been notably reduced. Mankind was beginning to be air-minded.

CHAPTER 2

The Air in the 1930's

As THE years immediately after World War I were the days of the air gypsies and the barnstormers, so the late 1920's and early 1930's could be called the "wildcat" period of aviation in the United States. They were years of airline promotion, bankruptcy, reorganization, and all the trimmings which go with young and spectacular industries in such an economy as ours.

Of 48 airlines in existence in 1929, for example, no less than 16 were out of business by the first of January 1930. During 1930 new flotations brought the total of American operating lines up to 45 again, but of these, 7 discontinued service before the end of the year. Many mail contractors were operating at a loss. Keen competition for passenger traffic saw rates cut so fine that it was often impossible for operators to make money, yet when fares were boosted passenger travel dwindled.

The Watres Act, passed by Congress in 1930, did much toward putting domestic air transportation in the United States on a sound footing, however. It gave the Postmaster General authority to unify the industry and, as a result, the next two years witnessed establishment of several sound operations. As examples, three transcontinental lines were organized from the maze of short-haul passenger and mail-carrying companies. United Air Lines stemmed from the merging of Boeing, Pacific Air Transport, National Air Transport, and Varney Air Lines, and was given the northern transcontinental route. American Airways, which merged several other smaller operations, became the southern transcontinental carrier and Trans-Continental and Western put into operation a mid-continent service from coast to coast. In addition to these, Eastern Air Lines was licensed to serve the Atlantic Coast region and Northwest Airlines and Western Air Express were given routes in the Pacific region.

As a result of these mergers, each using mail contracts as its financial back-log, the total number of airlines in the United States had dropped to fourteen by 1932. Through this period notable improvements were made in airways and airports. Commercial aviation in the United States seemed to have found its niche at last. Then disaster struck.

In 1934 the operators were thrown into complete disorganization when the incoming Federal Administration, as the result of alleged collusion between mail-carriers and Post Office officials, canceled overnight all airmail contracts and ordered the Army to fly the mail. Such drastic action, at first blush, seemed likely to put many operators out of business, for the mails comprised a much higher percentage of their revenue than is the case today. But the end was not yet. The assumption of the job by the Army was followed almost immediately by a series of fatal accidents to pilots who obviously lacked the specialized training required by the task suddenly thrust upon them. Before long the Government was glad to return the carrying of the mails to private operators properly equipped, and to men who had been trained as specialists in mail flying.

Meanwhile the volume of domestic passenger business was increasing by leaps and bounds throughout the Union. Better aircraft were coming from the production lines, machines capable of much higher speeds. The average of eight or nine seats which had been standard in 1934, by 1938 had become twelve. The industry, both as regards manufacturing and transportation, began to acquire conservatism and stability and, therefore, was able to attract conservative investment capital. The overnight cancellation of airmail contracts and the resulting clean-up legislation also had the effect of teaching carriers that they could not afford to keep all their eggs in the airmail basket. Soon all the major air-carriers were conducting intensive education campaigns to bring more passenger traffic to the airlines. Finally the Civil Aeronautics Act of 1938, which set up a single governmental authority to exercise complete control over every phase of interstate aviation, brought into being and regulated a thoroughly organized and closely controlled air transportation system throughout the Republic. Aviation was growing up and becoming a serious-minded young man.

European aviation meanwhile continued to expand. In December 1931 Major Kingsford Smith inaugurated the England-Australia mail route and in January 1932 the England-to-Capetown mail run began. In 1933 Imperial Airways completed ten million miles of flying and in the same year airmail service was extended from England to Calcutta and on to Rangoon. Before the year was out Rangoon had become just another stopping point when the service was extended to Singapore.

The Atlantic still remained the one great gap in Britain's all-red network. In 1937, however, Imperial undertook a series of commercial survey flights over the northern route and in July of that year the four-engined flying boat *Caledonia* crossed from Ireland to Newfoundland in fifteen hours and eight minutes. A second survey flight was made later in the same month. In the opinion of the experts of that day, however, the North Atlantic route could be used only in the summer, due to the rigors of its winter weather. Yet three years later fleets of American-built bombers would be winging their way from Montreal to Britain via Newfoundland in winter as in summer, and soon thereafter to the Middle East and India. So much for the prophets! Aviation has never lacked people ready and willing to tell the world what it would *not* be able to do, people who are always convinced that its zenith has been reached.

Perhaps the most interesting of all Britain's aerial experiments in the years immediately prior to World War II was the introduction of composite aircraft on the Atlantic run; huge "mother ships" which took off the water carrying "baby ships" which were released in the air and sent on their way, the idea being to give a flying start to the baby ship, which had enough power to carry its load, once in the air, but not enough for a take-off when fully loaded. On July 20, 1938, *Mercury*, a component of the Short composite aircraft, crossed from Ireland to Montreal in twenty hours, the first non-stop flight to the Canadian metropolis. On October 6 of that year *Mercury* was released from its mother ship, *Maia*, over Dundee, Scotland, and flew non-stop almost exactly 6000 miles to alight in the mouth of the Orange River in South Africa. The plan was abandoned shortly afterwards, however, as being impracticable, as the baby ships could not carry economic pay-loads.

Britain's developments in aviation, then as always, tended to move in terms of Empire. So, too, with Holland and France. Germany, released from the severe restrictions imposed after World War I, had been able to corral control of many internal airlines in South America, as indirect and unofficial offshoots of the German-owned Lufthansa, and had embarked upon a scheme of infiltration by air which we have not completely destroyed at the time of this writing.

The British continued to extend their world services even after war had broken out again, although by that time American operators had outstripped them in the global field. On the eve of war, British Overseas Airways Corporation, generally known as BOAC, was established to take over the operation of Imperial and a second "chosen instrument," British Airways, and to be Britain's exclusive representative in the field of international flight. Italy's entry into the war in 1940 closed off the Mediterranean mail and passenger routes, but within a short period the distant end of the line was in operation again with service from Durban in South Africa north to Egypt and thence to India, the Malay States, Australia, and New Zealand. Pan-American, in the meantime, was operating Clipper service from the United States to Lisbon, as well as through the Caribbean Islands and South America, and across the Pacific. To co-ordinate this Lisbon operation, British and Dutch passenger aircraft provided shuttle service between the United Kingdom and Portugal, the Germans operating a similar service between Lisbon and Berlin.

Such was the nature of development of commercial aviation through the 1930's. Belatedly the United States had followed on England's heels and was winging its way across the oceans with its huge clipper-ships. The oceans had all been spanned. The world stood in the doorway leading to all-out global flight. In the main the development in the field of engineering tended to be to aircraft of increasing size and motive power, and a primary problem had revolved about the question of loading more people into one airplane and transporting them over long distances.

As the war approached, however, leaders in the field of intercontinental flight tended to begin to think in terms of shorter hops which would not require lifting such heavy loads of fuel. The discovery had been made that it is cheaper to carry high octane gasoline by ship, say to Bermuda and the Azores, and to make aircraft refueling stops at such intermediate bases, than it is for an airplane to take off from the United States with the tremendous weight of gasoline required for the non-stop journey. Perhaps we shall discover with the return of peace that the islands along our airways where the Clippers fly have again become man's most valued possessions, as they were in the days of the old-time clipper-ships.

CHAPTER 3

Uncle Sam Goes to Town

EARLIER chapters have stressed that in the early days of commercial aviation, the years of the 1920's, the United States lagged behind Britain, Holland, France, and even Germany in intercontinental aviation. The British, viewing the new means of rapid transit through Imperial-minded eyes, had gone all out, almost immediately after World War I, to subsidize and establish airways which would tie together Britain's widely spread Empire. In developing these projects Britain's own position in relation to geography furnished a tremendous natural advantage. Aircraft could fly from Britain to Australia, to India, or to the Cape of Good Hope in comparatively easy stages by using intermediate landing grounds in British territory. No other nation, or group of nations, enjoyed such facilities.

There was no "freedom of the air" in the birth-pain days of international flight. Absolute air sovereignty had been established as the guiding principle under which each nation controlled the air above its own soil. Aircraft of other nations not merely could not land on or take off from foreign soil without first receiving permission, but could not even fly across other peoples' territory without it, under peril of being shot down should they attempt to do so. Holland, with its rich but remote empire in the East Indies, always led the fight for freedom of the air. The British manifested little if any interest in the thesis. That was because the Dutch, on the one hand, needed free access to air bases between Holland and their empire in the East Indies. The British, on the other hand, could fly from the United Kingdom throughout the vast reaches of their Oriental and sub-equatorial possessions without trespassing upon the air of any alien nation if necessary, although their aircraft might be called upon to fly circuitous routes over short distances. That problem they were able to resolve by purely unilateral treaties.

This "readiness of access" was largely responsible for Britain's tremendous development during the first decade after World War I. No other nation, or group of interrelated nations, enjoyed anything comparable to it. In fact, the British nations, provided they are prepared to collaborate as partners in future air policy, still remain in the most completely favorable position of all in respect to landing facilities throughout the world except, perhaps, for one Pacific blind-spot.

Perhaps this is as good a point as any at which to make a brief comparison between suggested plans for the use of the air when peace returns. At the two extremities are what may be called "freedom of the air" (which the British prefer to speak of as "open sky") and "air sovereignty," a nationalistic term identical with "closed sky," the world's prewar concept. The former would give all men complete freedom to move about the world by air on their innocent occasions as they see fit. Commercial aircraft, regardless of nationality, would be free to land on and take off from airports anywhere in the world without giving notice, subject only to regulations of a non-discriminatory nature. The doctrine of "closed sky," on the other hand, restricts all travel into, out of, or over any country excepting with its government's indulgence. Under such a policy any unauthorized passage becomes an act of trespass. Prior to World War II the latter was the basic principle of international practice. We have never known freedom of the air. Whether that freedom is to exist after the present war, or whether it should or should not exist, is a subject reserved for more elaborate discussion in a later chapter.

The point to be made here—and it is the only reason for referring to the subject at this juncture—is that Britain was in a position almost immediately after World War I to push out the tentacles of the first intercontinental air services without encroaching in any great degree on the air above alien nations. She was not forced to devote years to negotiation, compromise, and the establishment of a labyrinth of reciprocal unilateral deals. Virtually all that was required was to come to terms with her own Dominions and Colonies.

The United States was not in so happy a position by any means. Fundamentally that is the reason why that great nation was much slower than Britain to establish itself in the field of international flight. When Uncle Sam did begin to move, however, he did so with characteristic American energy and, by the time World War II came along, had outstripped all competitors. Considering that this problem had to be resolved by the individual American operator, with little assistance from his own State Department, that individuals had to conclude what were virtually personal treaties with foreign nations, enabling American flagships to fly over, or to and from, those countries, the American achievement is without parallel in the history of global flight. It was a notable achievement, primarily that of Pan-American Airways, but it was not the sort of achievement we can afford to carry through into the Air Age.

The guiding spirit of Pan-Am was and is that bundle of human energy, Juan Trippe. During the early 1920's, when other pioneers were attempting to make the first ocean crossings in aircraft by no means built for such tasks, and while other American aviation enthusiasts were looking solely to the development of interstate transportation, Trippe was looking out beyond the borders of his own country and dreaming of the day when the American flag would fly all over the world on great multi-engined airplanes operating under his direction. The trend of events favored Trippe's ambition. Year by year American engineers were achieving new victories in the realm of aero-dynamics and soon would be building planes of a sturdiness comparable to that of huge railway locomotives. Safety factors were constantly increasing through the media of radio controls and accurate weather reporting.

In 1927, the year in which Lindbergh flew to Paris, Pan-American finally edged into the field of international flight from the United States, with the islands and coastal regions of the Caribbean Sea as its first theater of operations. In the beginning the Americans constantly encountered the problems of the closed sky policy. With plans completed for the institution of a service between the United States and Brazil, for example, Venezuela, with 600 miles of coast straddling Pan-Am's most economical route, refused permission to the Americans to establish any service utilizing Venezuela's air. The story is told of a celebration in honor of the country's dictator, the late General Juan Vicente Gomez, in the City of Caracas. While troops paraded through one of the city's public squares before a reviewing stand on which Gomez and his aides were posed, an airplane flew over and, as it passed above the heads of the heroes of the occasion, released thousands of flowers, which fluttered down over the reviewing stand. An aide exclaimed, "What a beautiful tribute!" To which the aging dictator replied, "They might just as easily have been bombs." The remark contained the whole essence of the "closed sky" way of thought.

Despite proddings from Washington, the Venezuelan Government continued to refuse Pan-Am access to its air, forcing the Americans to fly along the West Indian islands to Trinidad and the Guianas to reach their destinations. Finally, in 1930, Gomez' successor issued a temporary franchise.

Trippe expanded his service through South America during the early 1930's. At last Uncle Sam had one foot in the doorway of international commercial aviation.

The American method of development was wholly dissimilar to that by which the British had created their great network during the 1920's, yet it had the final effect of making Pan-American Uncle Sam's unofficial "chosen instrument." What happened was that Pan-American had "chosen itself," and having done so, battered down the doors of foreign opposition, whereas in the case of Imperial and, later, British Overseas Airways, the Government of the United Kingdom did the "choosing" and conducted all required negotiations with foreign powers to establish the British network.

Trippe wrote his own treaties. Elsewhere in the world, negotiations between governments resulted in reciprocal arrangements. Trippe, on the other hand, went out and made his own arrangements, meeting many rebuffs, but finally establishing Pan-American terminals on foreign soil. In the beginning, by all accounts, it was a rough and tumble business. It also was the logical end-result of American isolationism as applied to the air, a policy which left the United States completely without responsibility in the realm of external flight.

What all nations feared, of course, was the importance of the airplane as a military instrument. What the "sovereignty" policy tended to do, however, was to create the kind of ill-will which leads men to take up arms. Millions of people, of course, still thought in horse-and-buggy terms. Hence questions of what they regarded as national security took precedence over all others. The International Air Convention in Paris of 1928 held strictly to the thesis of national air sovereignty. Certainly the United States clung to such ideas throughout the between-wars years, for by its Air Commerce Act of 1926 and the successor Act of 1938, the Republic categorically asserted its own "complete and exclusive national sovereignty" in the air above its territory.

Despite all these restrictions, however, world-wide air routes were managing to be born. Prior to World War II, British Overseas Airways had established itself in 31 countries, the greater number of which, of course, were British Dominions, Colonies, or Protectorates; the Dutch "chosen instrument," KLM, held landing privileges in 27; Air France in 15, while Pan-Am topped the list with 38.

The sovereignty policy was productive of strange results. Turkey, for example, flatly refused to give passage or landing privileges to international commercial air carriers and by its attitude blocked all European operators from access to the short route to the East. Greece turned Turkey's stubborn nationalism to its own advantage by insisting that all airlines flying across the Mediterranean toward the Orient land at Athens. Reciprocally she wangled from the British permission for Greek carriers to institute air service to Malta and Cyprus. In the middle 1930's, by which time Pan-Am had reached out across the Pacific as far as Manila, the British refused Trippe the right to land at Hong Kong and so blocked his Clippers from the mainland of Asia. Pan-Am promptly countered by persuading the Portuguese to let them into near-by Macao. Whereupon the British relented and invited Trippe into Hong Kong. The United States Government, not to be outdone in the realm of sovereignty, refused to permit either the British or Dutch to carry their trans-Pacific services into Honolulu, which prevented BOAC and KLM from reaching either the United States or Canada across the Pacific Ocean from the Orient, Britain's one major "blind-spot" area. But this was not all. The Australians promptly denied Pan-Am entry to the southern continent, but New Zealand gave Trippe landing and loading rights at Auckland.

From this the reader will readily accept the statement that national aerial conduct of the between-wars years was reminiscent of that of spoiled brats and was designed to engender hard feelings even between nations which normally live in pleasant and peaceful association, the logical outcome of all selfish nationalism. Two groups of world operators had come into being as a result of the national sovereignty policy. The four great European air carriers —BOAC (Britain), Air France, Lufthansa (German), and KLM (Holland)—worked in close co-operation as to routes, traffic arrangements, and schedules. The French pooled with the Germans on the South American routes, with the Dutch to the Far East, and in some degree with the Belgians into Africa. As opposed to these co-operative arrangements, the United States, the Soviet Union, Turkey, China, and Japan either discouraged or directly forbade international operations into or over their territories. The essence of these policies was their extreme selfishness, arrant nationalism, and dog-eat-dog outlook. Pray God we do not make the mistake of returning to it!

As opposed to these modes of procedure, Pan-American Airways, through the hard-driving personality of Trippe, literally forced its way into the arena of intercontinental flight, not merely from the United States to South America, but to Europe and across the Pacific, through the medium of a series of unilateral agreements, personally negotiated. Pan-Am's European service actually was initiated only ten weeks before the outbreak of war in the autumn of 1939, by which time Trippe was getting his first taste of competition from home. Not all his fellow-American operators were going to sit back and let the young tornado from Pan-Am pick up all the juicy plums.

First to attempt invasion of Trippe's territory was the newly formed (1939) American Export Airlines which sought a license from the Civil Aero Board in Washington to fly from the United States to various European points. Thus was the first home-front airline war in Pan-Am's stormy history born. American Export's original application was to institute an experimental fortnightly round trip to an unnamed European terminal and they requested a $500,000 annual Post Office subsidy for mail service—a bagatelle by comparsion with sums being paid to Pan-American for carrying the mails. Export accused Pan-Am of operating a throttling monopoly and charged Trippe with directing one of the smoothest lobbies in Washington. The fur flew in clouds and Export appeared to have won the first round when it emerged with a permit from Washington to fly to Lisbon. It was a short-lived victory, for when Export made the next move to establish its transocean route, its directors suddenly discovered that Pan-Am had already tied down exclusive rights in the Azores and Portugal for aircraft of American registry for a quarter-century to come. That left Export on the far end of a limb, looking none too bright.

Trippe's rugged individualism, nothing else, literally forced open the doors of world aviation for Uncle Sam. The European nations, on the other hand, had made their way through policies of international compromise and negotiation. Each method, it could be said, was typical of the people who employed it.

CHAPTER 4

The Bush-Fliers

WAS the creation of intercity, international, and intercontinental airways the be-all and end-all of aviation's between-wars record? By no means.

While civil aviation and commercial flight were feeling their first growing pains in the United States and Europe, Canada and Canadian air pioneers were engaged in projects which clearly pointed out many of the especial commercial potentialities of flight. What is more, those Canadian pioneers acquired a knowledge of winter flying under Arctic and sub-Arctic conditions which was to prove invaluable in cracking open the North Atlantic for winter bomber-deliveries in a world again at war.

The reference is to what has become generally known as "bush-flying," in this case the opening of the great spaces of the Canadian North through the medium of the airplane and the development of its mineral wealth, its fur and fish trade, over an area reaching to the Arctic Circle and from Labrador to the Yukon. It was a different kind of development to that which took place anywhere else. It was undertaken by hardy adventurous spirits, most of whom began with no capital but their own courage, faith in the country, and a couple of elderly aircraft tied together with bits of baling wire.

Each project *had* to pay its way; otherwise the operator might be out of business at the end of any thirty-day period. Its fundamental revenue was always freight, whereas in the United States and Europe the first job of the pioneers of commercial flight was to destroy the ordinary man's fear of leaving the ground, a long-term program which involved the operator's ability to take losses over a lengthy period of public education. In Canada, however, the reverse was the case, because the operator was offering to deliver the human being and his chattels, or, say, his mining machinery, to points often so far removed from rail or other communications as to involve weeks of dog-team or canoe travel as the only alternative. Under such conditions, obviously, the opening of the rich Canadian North was impossible. Then the bush-flier came along and wrought the miracle.

The first flight of note in Canada after the war took place on October 7, 1919, when Captain Ernest Hoy crossed the Rockies west-bound, from Lethbridge to Vancouver, in sixteen hours and forty-five minutes—a longer time than that which elapses in fast crossings of the Atlantic from America to Europe today.

The first serious venture in hinterland flying was undertaken in 1920 by Imperial Oil Limited—Canadian cousin to Standard —which acquired two Junkers low-wing all metal monoplanes to open rapid transit communication between the railway and its oil wells at Fort Norman, close to the Arctic Circle on the MacKenzie River, later to be the source of supply of the great Canol project.

The town of Peace River was chosen as the southern base and a route laid out to follow the Peace River to a point near Fort Vermillion, thence across country to the western end of Great Slave Lake and north down the MacKenzie River to Fort Norman.

The two Junkers set out from Peace River on March 24, 1921, and reached Fort Simpson on the MacKenzie where they were grounded by a combination of engine trouble and ski and propeller breaks. A month passed while the crews were making repairs, by which time the long northern winter was on the point of breaking up. Therefore the two pilots, Elmer Fullerton and George Gorman, deciding that discretion is sometimes still the better part of valor, headed south without having reached Fort Norman's oil wells. Imperial soon abandoned its project.

What may be termed the first serious attempt to establish scheduled passenger, mail, and freight services by air came in 1924. A great gold rush was in progress in what has since become the Rouyn camp, the home of many thriving mines, amongst them Noranda, one of the world's richest deposits of copper and gold. Today Rouyn is a prosperous urban community connected to the outside world by two lines of railway. But in the early 1920's it was a high, wide, and handsome boom camp, cut off from Canada's nearest populated areas by 200 miles of forests and swamps, threaded by a single turbulent river. In 1924, however, a couple of daredevils who had flown with distinction overseas, and who had acquired a couple of Curtiss Jennies after coming home, decided to offer freight and passenger service to prospectors, geologists, and engineers who might prefer to risk their necks in the air rather than face the long Kinojevis River haul with its many portages. The scheme was a success from its inception. That year Laurentide Air Service carried 1004 passengers, 15,000 letters, and 78,000 pounds of freight into the newly staked gold fields. In the same year the Canadian Government contracted with the same operators to fly the annual Treaty Money to the Indian tribes along the shores of James Bay. The flights were made without mishap, covering a circuit more than 1000 miles in circumference. The Treaty Money flights continue to this day.

In 1925 two famous Canadian bush-flying pioneers, Caldwell and Scott-Williams, made the first major prospecting flight. Starting from Prince Rupert, British Columbia, in a Vickers Viking amphibian, they went north along the coast as far as Wrangel where they turned inland, crossed the coastal range, and flew up the Stikine Valley to Telegraph Creek. There they were forced to wait for ice to leave the rivers and lakes. On June 3 they moved farther inland to Dease Lake, where they dismounted the amphibian's wheels and carried on into the Liard country, using their ship as a flying-boat and maintaining Dease Lake as their base. They shuttled back and forth, carrying geologists and prospectors into the mountains from Dease, until July when they moved their base forward to Liard, from which point they operated through August, dropping and picking up prospecting parties for the mining syndicate to which they were under contract. That was the beginning of aerial prospecting, not merely in Canada but anywhere in the world.

By this time the mining community had come to see the value of aerial transportation into Canada's northern wilderness. The question of airdromes presented no problem, for the country is pocked with lakes ranging in size from inland seas to frog-ponds. Aircraft shod with pontoons in summer and with skis in winter were seldom out of gliding range to safe landings. The pioneer bush-fliers, of course, had no radio communication with their bases and radio stations were not established in the mining settlements until well into the 1930's. Once a plane left "the tracks" (the nearest railway base) with its load of passengers or supplies, it was gone from human ken until it came homing out of the north. Fatal accidents were few, however, for the bush-fliers, knowing themselves to be at the mercy of the elements, flew with care. The freights they carried inbound were of tremendous value, comprising all manner of machinery, sometimes even live cows and horses. Outbound they brought precious bullion, radium-ore concentrates from Great Bear Lake, fish and furs. The idea was to deliver the goods, eschewing all unnecessary risks. Hence it was the fliers' habit, on running into bad weather, of the approach of which they seldom had warning, to get down onto the nearest lake and sit it out. The Canadian bush-fliers, in short, were the first flying "small-businessmen," and they flew like businessmen, taking no unnecessary chances.

Soon the Canadian North was dotted with bush airlines, each of which had one foot on the railway and the other in some northern mining camp, sometimes as distant as 1000 miles from the nearest civilized community. In those days, as you traveled across Canada by rail, seaplanes riding at anchor on lakes beside the railway line and waiting to load materials for the Far North were to be seen at wilderness-sidings by the score. In the Province of Quebec the bush-pilots were flying, as already noted, into the Rouyn country, into Chibougamau and northeast to Labrador. In Ontario the great Red Lake camp, into which the first aerial freighting of huge mining machinery was carried out before the mid-1920's, was connected by aircraft with the railway line at Sioux Lookout. The town of Red Lake soon became a thriving modern community, equipped with electric light and running water, schools and housing, with every amenity of a modern American town. Yet the nearest highway and railway station were more than 100 miles to the south. In Manitoba the airplane opened up God's Lake and many other camps. When Gilbert Labine discovered radium deposits at Great Bear Lake, astride the Arctic Circle, he did so by virtue of having been dropped in the country by Leigh Brintnell, one of Canada's best-known northern fliers, who left the prospector in the north all summer and came back to meet him at an appointed rendezvous in the fall. By the time pilot and prospector had kept their autumn rendezvous, Labine had found pitchblende and the world's greatest single source of radium was ready to be made available to humanity.

Great Bear Lake is still many hundreds of miles from the railway at Fort McMurray, Alberta. For two or three months during the summer it can be reached by water, over the Athabaska and Slave Rivers from McMurray, with one long portage at Fort Smith, whence barges and shallow-draft steamers move on through the northern reaches of the Slave onto Great Slave Lake and down the

MacKenzie to a point near Fort Norman, where they turn into the rapids-ridden Bear River up which they are man-handled into Great Bear Lake. It is an arduous journey and the season is short. But men and supplies are carried by air from Edmonton or Fort McMurray in a day.

Thanks to the airplane modern living conditions were soon established about the radium workings at Great Bear. As at Red Lake the miners soon enjoyed steam heat, running water, shower baths, and electric light. Even fresh meat and vegetables are flown across almost 1000 miles of barren tundra to feed them. An engineer can step into the cabin of the company-owned airplane on the Arctic Circle at daybreak, clad in parka, high boots, and all the strange gear of the arctic winter. Evening may see him dining in his club in Edmonton, complete with dinner jacket and black tie. Not particularly surprising today, perhaps, when men breakfast in London and dine in Washington. But it was no small trick in the early 1930's.

For years the bush-fliers and their only serious sponsors, the men of the mining industry, struggled against almost insuperable odds. The Canadian Government, which like most others persistently refused to take aviation seriously, provided few facilities and little help to the fliers. The business had to stand on its own feet or perish, for the politicians had not then realized the importance of tapping the great mineral resources of the Far North. The fliers struggled on. Some of them went broke and tried again. Others got by from month to month and year to year. If mining struck a slump, northern aviation went to perdition with it. The people in Canada who were then involved in aviation were involved for only one reason—they would be damned if they would get out of it. This was their life and nothing on earth was going to make them live any other.

What may be called the first "responsible" Canadian money to be poured into northern commercial aviation came in 1926 when H. A. (Doc) Oaks, one of the bush pioneers, persuaded the late James A. Richardson, millionaire Winnipeg grain man, to put up enough money to weld together a group of detached northern airlines. Richardson was a far-seeing and adventurous man, imbued with a deep love of Canada. With Oaks he formed and financed what came to be known as Western Canada Airways, bought a couple of Fokker Universals, and promptly demonstrated the feasibility of back-country flying by carrying several tons of supplies and a number of construction and technical experts to Churchill on the Hudson Bay coast, now the terminus of the Hudson Bay Railroad, the route for which was then being surveyed.

Western Canada soon extended its operations throughout the Northwest, taking any business which was offered, from anywhere to anywhere. When fur traders operating north of the Arctic Circle in the Northwest Territories were urgently in need of money but could not get their furs out and convert them into cash, they went to Richardson for help. Jim sent his pilots into the country, brought out bale after bale of valuable furs in a few days, enabling the traders to sell them in a good market whereas, had they been forced to wait for the normal means of transportation to bring the furs out, a year later, the goods would have been sold in a collapsed market, at prices below the cost of trapping, shipment, and preparation.

In the late 1920's the Canadian Government began to dabble in airmail contracts for the isolated camps, notably the Red Lake and Central Manitoba mines. In the East mails were being flown down the isolated North Shore of the St. Lawrence, east of Quebec, and to the Magdalen Islands, off the coast of New Brunswick. In summer seaplanes met incoming steamers in the Gulf of St. Lawrence, picked up the mails, and carried them ashore, speeding up letter deliveries from England to Canada by two days. At last, after much pushing and prodding by the airmen, the Government was beginning to realize how great a contribution the bush-fliers were making to the opening of the North.

Richardson now induced the authorities to establish airmail across the country along its populated strip, most of which lies within 100 miles of the Canadian-United States boundary. A beginning was made between Toronto and Montreal. Then it was decided to fly the Prairies west from Winnipeg to the eastern foothills of the Rockies. Soon the country was covered from coast to coast, excepting the wilderness north of Lake Superior and the mountainous country between the Prairies and the Pacific coast. In the East the mails were flown by day, thrown aboard trains for the run around the upper Great Lakes, carried across the prairies by air during the night, then transported through the Rockies to finish the journey by rail. Thus was the size of Canada contracted by the airplane.

Year by year the smaller airlines merged. Mail services were extended and the country began to acquire air-mindedness. But nobody was making a dollar and it is a reasonable bet that Richardson poured at least a million dollars of his own money into aerial pioneering and never took a penny out.

Nevertheless Canada had pioneered an entirely new field of flight. Fort McMurray, 300 miles north of Edmonton, became the greatest freight and express airport in the world, with thirty or forty landings and as many take-offs in a day. The Canadian back-country fliers had opened a vast region millions of square miles in extent to natural resource development which otherwise would have laid fallow for generations, perhaps for centuries. In Northern Canada journeys which involved weeks, sometimes months, of arduous travel on the ground were brought into civilization's back-yard by the northern airlines.

The experience acquired has been of unassessable value in war. When the first transatlantic ferry between North America and Britain was established in 1940, it was to a former Canadian bush-pilot and World War I veteran, Captain C. H. (Punch) Dickins, that the task of organizing what was then regarded as a most hazardous and risky job was entrusted. The British were prepared to lose at least 10 per cent of the bombers bound from American factories to the war fronts of Europe, but deemed the risk less than the hazards of shipment by sea. Until then aircraft earmarked for Britain had been dismantled at the eastern seaboard, carried by ship to England and reassembled for battle on the other side, involving a time lag of weeks, often months, for those which reached their destination. But Dickins brought into the Ferry Command with him the nucleus of a flying organization composed of veteran Canadian bush-pilots and ex-American-airline captains. The bush-pilots brought to their task a knowledge of the hazards of northern flight possessed by no other group of men in the world. Their colleagues from the United States brought other qualifications. At no time in the history of transatlantic ferrying have losses ever reached 1 per cent. But of this, more anon. Suffice to say here that the knowledge and special skills of the Canadian bush-fliers were of inestimable value in cracking open the North Atlantic and, therefore, played a role of high importance in solving Britain's post-blitz aircraft problem.

Moreover the Canadian North Country fliers, by their example, had brought the possibilities of flight into isolated places to the attention of the rest of the aviation world. It is not beyond reason to say that it is from their storehouse of experience that we have drawn the military knowledge which has made possible the carrying of troops and supplies into isolated war areas, such as Burma and China, to which large bodies of men have been transported and supplied from the air. No greater contribution to the world's knowledge of flight has been made than that of the Canadian bush-fliers. All honor to a gallant band!

CHAPTER 5

Germany's Geopolitical Aviation

THE Peace Conference temporarily erased Germany as an air power, the object of those who wrote the Treaty undoubtedly being to make the erasure permanent. In that outlook they counted without the brilliant cupidity of the Germans and our own stupidity, which permitted Germany to reintrude into the realm of military aviation, with the result that, almost before our leaders knew it and certainly without that knowledge reaching down to the people of the democracies, our enemies were well on the way to being ready to strike again in the air.

On the surface the German policy was innocent enough. The Allies had seen to it that the enemy should be denied the use of high-powered, heavier-than-air machines, but overlooked completely the fact that gliding is also aviation, and that the pilot who has learned to glide only needs an engine to be able to do everything else in the bright lexicon of flight. So the Germans took to gliding, and glider groups, clubs, and schools were established throughout the Reich while the victors were squabbling about matters relating to commerce in the air and practically paying no attention to their military responsibilities. That was the beginning of German rearmament and it happened almost before the ink was dry on the Treaty of Versailles. Thus while America was withdrawing into isolation and the rest of us were pretending to equip the League of Nations with store teeth (with very little vestige of success because of the constant intrusion of everybody's national selfishness), the Germans, under the influence of their geopoliticians, already were preparing for the second war in the air.

Throughout Germany in the years immediately following World War I, youngsters were gliding all over the skies in every spare hour they could find. Thousands of them were lads no older than today's air cadets, but while our school boys were still restricted to drilling on the ground and to classroom study on such subjects as Theory of Flight, the young German of the early 1920's was flying gliders. What is more, he knew, even then, what he was flying about. He was learning to fly with one object in view, the coming of *Der Tag*, the day when the sons of Germany would turn on their enemies and drive them from the skies of the world. In addition, the German youngster was being converted, even in his teens and long before Hitler, into an expert geopolitician. As a corollary to instruction in gliding and preparation for deeper exploration in the realm of flight, his teachers in the schools were hammering into his young head a picture of a world in which Germany would seize her place in the sun and become at last the dominant factor in the shaping of a new order.

It is senseless to view the military renaissance of the German people as Hitler's personal invention. The renaissance was conceived in the minds of Germans everywhere no later than the morning of the 12th of November 1918, and by the time the Versailles Treaty was down on paper the German people were marching again toward the day of revenge. Hitler was merely their instrument, the man who turned to his own purposes the spirit of the German nation, its desire for expansion, and its determination to be avenged, and gave to that spirit its valid form. He, or his propagandists, may have invented such stirring phrases as "master race." He may have found the method by which to unite all groups and classes in Germany. He may have been the force which destroyed such opposition as existed and he may have been the instrument which defied the world and finally forced us to arm (after we had helped him to do so) and our cringing leaders to take up the sword. But the seeds were present throughout the period. Hitler merely tended them, raised the crop, and garnered it. Let us hope that when the day comes to put down on paper once more a concept of world law and order, we shall remember the role played by the German nation, not merely from the coming of Adolf Hitler, but from the sound of the "cease fire" in 1918. There can be no living in the same world with Germany until her people know in the depths of their souls the folly and futility of their dreams of world conquest.

Proof of that spirit was to be seen in many directions. Many of us who had been flying during World War I and who had continued our association with aviation into the days of peace knew only too well what was going on. But to know and to obtain a hearing in responsible political quarters for our views was without avail. The politicians saw in the retaking to the air of German youth, via the glider, nothing more serious than an innocent amusement, whereas the old war fliers knew that what was occurring was the rebirth of Germany's military aviation.

Not all our leaders lived in that strange *galère*. In Britain Winston Churchill was constantly on the *qui vive*, constantly telling the nation to keep her eye on Germany, and being dubbed a war monger for his pains. He and I discussed the problem of the air together more than once when I was in Britain in the early 1920's. Neither of us was "cured." Each of us believed that civilized mankind still had Germany to reckon with and that the side which controlled the air would win the next war. In the United States my dear friend General Billy Mitchell was perhaps the most clear-sighted of all the believers in air-power—and everybody knows what happened to Mitchell—a grateful nation kicked him out of the service for his views and his determination to make them heard. The trouble with us—and by "us" I mean the United States and the nations of the British Commonwealth—is that we can win wars, belatedly choosing the right weapons, but completely lack the flair for making Victory stick.

While the outlook of other nations in the realm of aviation during the greater part of the period between wars was largely commercial and tended latterly to become commercial in the global sense, the whole German approach was always fundamentally military and geopolitical. Banned from the production of military aircraft and armaments, German interests soon were subsidizing private manufacturers in such countries as Sweden, Belgium, and France, whose factories immediately became the workshops of German designers and engineers. There was subsidization, too, of aerial armament works, such as those of Bofors and Oerlikon in other European countries. The Germans were waiting for the day when they would be able to wheedle us into letting them back into the air, whence it would be but a short step into actual military flying. In the meantime, however, they were not letting the grass grow under their feet, but were making use of the cupidity of manufacturers outside Germany to keep German military aviation abreast, or ahead, of the times. They knew that the day would come soon when the democracies would let down the barriers. If necessary, the Germans would even provide a plausible reason for doing so, and in due course they did. Its name was Russia. Remember?

The 1920's were not far spent before we decided that it would be unfair to refuse our dear German ex-enemies the right to fly commercially on virtually the same terms as those which we ourselves enjoyed. From this policy stemmed the Lufthansa aerial network in Europe, which quickly spread its tentacles beyond continental borders and began to share with Britain, France, Holland, and other nations the leading positions in world commercial aviation; this while the United States was still virtually without organized domestic airways and long before the entry of Uncle Sam into the field of intercontinental flight.

The Germans did not stop there. By the beginning of the 1930's Germany had become the aviation aggressor in South America. She had not only linked that continent to Europe, via Lufthansa, but had established a chain of German-owned airlines throughout the South American continent. These, of course, functioned under dummy ownership and ostensibly were native enterprises, but behind the façade of South American directorship always hid the German bankroll and the corps of efficient German air and ground personnel. Many of these German dummy airlines operated at constant financial loss in sparsely settled regions. Rates were kept low. Germany was developing its politico-economic policy and developing a system of airfields and communications in South America which would prove highly useful as and when she would be ready to squeeze the United States from the South.

By the time Poland was invaded in 1939, Germany and her friends controlled 20,000 miles of airlines in the Western Hemisphere alone. Pan-American at that time had only 15,000, and its affiliate, Panair do Brazil, less than 10,000. The Germans owned Sindicato Condor, Ferig, and Vasp in Brazil. In Bolivia they had Lloyd Anso Boliviano. Sedta in Ecuador was theirs. They had Scadta in Colombia, Lati and Aero-Posta in Argentina. Even though these dummy lines were outlawed shortly after the European war began, only the most skillful and high-pressure diplomacy could make their final outlawry stick. Here, then, was the hub of the German air policy between the two wars. While the democracies were completely engrossed with private commerce, as in the United States, or with the establishing of Empire networks, as in Britain, the German outlook remained that of military conquest, the business of making ready for the day when she would rise up again against the world.

Consider the visit of von Gronau to North America toward the end of the 1920's. Other aviators had flown to these shores from Europe on peaceful missions. The others had been adventurers, trail-blazers. Similarly when fliers from the democratic countries pushed their way into the domestic aviation of other lands they did so in the belief that an honest dollar could be turned and they were not politically backed from home. But a respectable commerce, or high adventure for its own sake, as already noted, were never the purposes which took German operators (excepting, perhaps, von Huenefeld, who was a gay character) afield.

Nor was the making of a contribution of value to world aviation the purpose which brought von Gronau across the Atlantic in his Dornier-Wahl flying-boat. Whereas a British or American trail-blazing Atlantic flier flew because he wanted to win a big prize, or perhaps to sell the story of his adventures to a group of American newspapers for a large sum of money, von Gronau and his crew flew solely to blaze a potential trail for German military aviation over the North Atlantic route. He flew the great circle into Greenland, where a few years later the United Nations encountered considerable difficulty in kicking German weather-scientists off that Atlantic stepping stone. Probably it was von Gronau who brought home the basic information as to how Greenland might be used.

Stops were made in Labrador and Newfoundland before the Germans landed in Canada. The subsequent visit to Chicago was probably only camouflage for their real purpose, a survey of the great circle routes by air. Von Gronau carried on northwest across Canada, over the Great Lakes and the Northwest Territories, with stops at strategic points en route. Is it possible that the German fliers even then decided on the sites of fuel caches that the Royal Canadian Mounted Police were to uncover years later when Germany and Canada were again at war? Von Gronau's journey which brought him to Tokyo was geopolitical just as the German approach has been geopolitical since the day on which the Treaty of Versailles was signed. Every move, every action of Germany's leaders, and of those who followed Germany's leaders, long before Hitler appeared, has had the one driving force of revenge and conquest behind it.

Any comparison of our and Germany's aviation outlooks between World War I and World War II may leave us able to say that we had no thought of aggrandizement, but it also leaves us looking like extremely stupid people.

Germany recognized the importance of the air in war, as in

making ready for war, by making the *Luftwaffe* the senior service, in spite of its youth. Even before the Germans openly possessed any military aviation between the two wars, the Reich maintained in its service the great majority of its experienced airmen and they became the leaders of preparation for the renewing of hostilities. Under Goering these men organized the German air force with such flexibility as to enable its whole weight to be concentrated on any desired area at the shortest notice. They gave it unity of command and operational control. They organized its offensive forces entirely separately from those which are primarily non-offensive and gave to the offensive arm extreme mobility. They brought to Germany's air-power unity of command and an intelligence of direction which were not paralleled in any Allied air force, primarily because the politico-military direction of the Western Democracies was not only not air-minded but in some cases was jealously anti-air.

The *Luftwaffe* maintained operational control of all German military aircraft excepting those which were shipborne. Grouped with the air-power control were anti-aircraft and air-raid precaution forces. Offensive or striking forces were organized into air-striking commands, the mobility of which was maintained by making the actual flying forces of each command detachable from their ground headquarters. Headquarters organization remained virtually static, the flying force highly mobile. In other words, the Germans very early in the business of fighting air wars recognized that if you encumber the fastest of all weapons by saddling it with cumbersome ground organization, you will slow it down and lessen its striking power. The British countries and the United States, on the other hand, long after becoming involved in World War II, sacrificed mobility to administrative encumbrances. That the United Nations finally were able to take the offensive in virtually every theater of war and to exercise sovereignty over our own and the enemy's air, was not due to any brilliant concept in their political organization for war, but to the superlative production of our aircraft factories (particularly those of the United States), to the fact that the greater part of our production was beyond the reach of our enemies' weapons while we were able to strike stinging blows at their production, to our development of a round-the-world aircraft delivery system, and, above all, to the gallantry and dash of our young men.

The real concept of aviation's power as an instrument of war was Germany's, not ours. It gave our enemies advantage over us for more than three years. Similarly Germany's geopolitical aviation outlook between the two air wars, as opposed to our insistence upon regarding flight either from the point of view of the adventurer on one hand, or the money-grubber on the other, gave the Germans two strikes over the democracies. Fortunately for us, in the final decision old-line Junker Generals were still able to force some of their views on Hitler and to keep the airplane at least partially tied to the panzers, or God alone knows how serious the rout might have become. It was too close a shave as it was.

PART IV

Ordeal by Air

CHAPTER 1

Germany Strikes Again

BEFORE considering the reasons why Germany's offensive in the air during World War II succeeded in its first phases, almost succeeded completely, and failed in the end, we should consider the state of world aviation at the time of the invasion of Poland in 1939. In the first place, the general run of western mankind was becoming air-minded. Aircraft had achieved a stability and degree of safety favorably comparable to that of any other means of transportation. Scientific aids to flight were many and varied. Internal airlines crisscrossed every populated area of Europe, the Americas, much of Asia, and the remote continents. Huge clipper-ships and luxury airliners winged across the oceans of the world. In some degree, at least, global flight had become part of the pattern of man's daily life.

The general opinion among laymen appears to have been that the peak had been scaled. The immense new vistas which have been opened during the second world war in aviation's brief but dramatic lifetime were not realized even by many of those who had been closely identified with the developments of the 1930's. In so far as we in the democracies dreamed of the future at all in the last summer of peace, it was of one in which larger and more luxurious airliners might ultimately ply from continent to continent, possibly, but not probably, in competition with the steamship in economy of operation. When a group of Russian aviators whisked across the polar regions and down our Pacific coast, few people realized that the Soviet fliers were blazing a trail soon to be a traveled air highway which would change the whole aspect of our geographical thinking.

Similarly when Britain, the United States, and Canada met in London brief months before the outbreak of World War II and solemnly put forward the view that the North Atlantic is not climatically conducive to safe winter flying, few people realized how foolish such pronouncements would appear against the record about to be compiled by the young men who would establish a non-stop shuttle service over that bleak and dismal waste and beyond it to anywhere-in-the-world before two winters were out.

Yet there were some who knew what the Russian flight meant, and who must have properly evaluated the solemn pronouncements made at the London Conference. On the other side of the Rhine, thought had followed the curved lines of global geography for two decades. Germany knew fully that the first step toward achievement of her geopolitical ambitions must be taken in the air—and she was prepared to take it.

It has been said that Nazi aerial blitzkrieg tactics took the world by surprise. Such a statement is made, of course, for the purpose of exonerating those who thought they could avert war with Hitler through the medium of diplomatic negotiation. They were men so steeped in outmoded ideas of warfare on the one hand or consumed by their reverence for the sanctity of trade rather than of people on the other, that they neglected to arm against the clearly obvious threat of barbaric attack from across the Rhine.

Actually the coming of the blitz was about as secret as the presence of the sun in the sky. What was wrong was that we had failed, and failed dismally, to shoulder the responsibilities of the task which we knew we must face or give up our freedom. If anybody was surprised by the blitzing of country after country it could only have been the species of person who was surprised by Hitlerian double-crossing before and after Munich. It is useless at this juncture to launch any new denouncements of the collaborationists in our own ranks in Britain, the British Commonwealth, and the United States. But the only surprise of the blitzkrieg was the surprise accorded to the few people who ever believed that Hitler's signature made a contract binding. Nobody but those wishful thinkers, the sincere Appeasers, ever believed that.

Several factors came within the proverbial hair's breadth of bringing us to our doom. The first was the political factor, the policy of Appeasement and its ugly godchild, quasi-Fascism at home. The second was the stubbornness of our old-fashioned military men who clung steadfastly to the ideas of warfare in vogue before the coming of the airplane, despite the lessons which aviation should have taught them between 1914 and 1918. Still another was the school of seagoing thought which continued to regard oceans as natural barriers against invasion and its corollary, belief in the almightiness of the super-battleship.

By this time it is to be hoped we have learned, via the school of hard knocks, that all our preconceived notions of warfare are as dead as the dodo.

France had believed that a long line of fortifications ending against the Belgian border (as if an imaginary line could establish an insurmountable obstacle) rendered her safe from invasion. Yet the Maginot Line would have been almost equally useless had it reached across Belgium to the Channel. The *Luftwaffe* would simply have played leap-frog over it and taken it from behind. Similarly in Britain old-line military men prepared for another war of blockade and attrition, presumably to be fought in trench systems, as in 1914–1918, and from such "impregnable fortresses" as Singapore; all of which would have been excellent if only our enemies would have agreed to fight according to the recognized rules. So, too, with Uncle Sam, whose detection devices were not even in operation when the Japs descended upon Pearl Harbor. Such things were fancy gew-gaws to the old-fangled military man. The truth of the matter is that not one of the democracies as a whole (there were a few air-minded individuals within them who did) grasped the implications of the air in war until our enemies taught us our lesson the hard way.

The invasion of Poland removed some of our political mildew. But the land-borne blitz against Europe and the collapse of the Maginot Line, spearheaded by hordes of Stukas, failed to erase the belief that modern wars can be won by attrition, although it did help to get rid of some of the military men who held them. Japan's amazing leap-frogging movement across the Pacific and our losses of capital ships at sea, because they were without air protection, plus the havoc wrought at Pearl Harbor, taught at least *some* naval men that not only are the oceans *not* barriers but are ready-made stepping stones for the use of aggressors who know the importance of the marriage of sea- and air-power, a marriage in which the air element has become the dominant partner. It has taken a long time to learn our lesson.

Fortunately, we were not the only blunderers. Germany still had its handful of ground-bound generals who, although they knew the value of the *Luftwaffe's* striking power, saw it primarily as a weapon to be used in short thrusts to clear the way ahead for ground forces and to terrorize civilian populations. There were men in Germany who disagreed with the old Junkers, who saw the real value of the airplane as a weapon. They would have given the *Luftwaffe* heavier armament with which to meet its enemies in the air. They would have given the German bomber greater carrying capacity in death-dealing missiles. But, fortunately for us, Hitler and Goering listened to the generals and compromised between the land-bound men and the men of the air, perhaps to keep peace in the inner circle. That blunder is one for which we can thank our lucky stars. As in Germany, so in Britain, but our mistakes were of somewhat different caliber. Our airmen were at least able to make their voices heard to the point that they could give us fighter aircraft and fighting airmen capable of routing the enemy in the skies. We could never have driven the Germans off in the Battle of Britain if our fighter aircraft had not been superior to any which the Germans could bring to the attack. Our mistake was that we did not have enough men or machines, a circumstance which almost encompassed our defeat in spite of Germany's blunders. Thus, though in different ways, the air-minded people were not given full rein on either side in the early years of this war. Had this been otherwise in Germany, but not in Britain, Britain would have fallen; had it been otherwise in Britain, but not in Germany, Hitler might have lost the war in the first year. But the mistakes occurred on each side and they were the mistakes of men trapped by tradition. So they canceled each other out.

What was the weakness of the German aircraft which attacked Britain after the fall of France, through the medium of which Germany already had subjugated all that part of Europe which lies to the west of the Third Reich? If the *Luftwaffe* could do the first job, why did it fail in the second?

The two primary bombers used by the Nazis against Britain were the Junkers 87, the Stuka dive-bomber, and its twin-engined mate, the Junkers 88. The former made its appearance in Poland and then in Western Europe in a most fearsome manner. Equipped with sirens which shrieked terrifyingly as the attacking aircraft bore down on fleeing armies and civilians, it spread death and destruction in the van of the mechanized spearheads which followed on the ground and which completed the occupation of air-invaded areas. It succeeded over the mainland of Europe primarily because of lack of opposition. Once it turned to England and came to grips with the Hurricane and the Spitfire, the reputation of the awe-inspiring Stuka was quickly punctured and destroyed, simply because Germany had sacrificed armament and armor to speed. The Stuka carried two fixed machine guns in the wings and one other machine gun in the rear cockpit. It was entirely unprotected against attack from underneath and when attacked from the rear had only one light machine gun with which to ward off the eight guns which the British single-seater fighter could bring to bear. That is why Germany littered the ground of Britain with destroyed Stukas during the blitz. If Britain had only had more Hurricanes and Spitfires, and more fighter pilots to fly them, the *Luftwaffe* would have been wiped out, or would have been forced to withdraw from the field sooner than it did.

The Junkers 88 was twin-engined, carrying a crew of four at a speed of approximately 300 miles an hour, and possessed greater range than the Stuka, which dare not exceed a radius of more than 200 miles from its base. In blitz days it carried three machine guns, one operated by a gunner in front of the pilot, the others astern, one above and the other below the body of the fuselage. It was no more effective than the Stuka.

Also used extensively in the Battle of Britain was the Heinkel 3, a twin-engined low-winged monoplane. A few Dornier 7's also were used. The characteristics of all these types were largely similar. All were fast, as speeds were judged at the beginning of the war. But speed had been obtained in each by sacrificing fighting ability, armor, and the ability to carry heavy bomb-loads. That was the primary factor in the defeat of the *Luftwaffe* over Britain—this and the fact that Britain's aircraft were really armed to fight.

The British Air Ministry in a pamphlet summing up the record of the Battle of Britain from August 8 to October 31, 1940, saw it as having taken place in four distinct phases.

(1) A concentrated attack was exerted on convoys in the Channel, on the coast line and harbors of southeastern Britain, and on airdromes located in Kent, Essex, and the vicinity of London from August 8 to the 18th.

(2) From August 19 to September 5 the *Luftwaffe* directed its full force against fighter airdromes inland, in the belief that by doing so it could destroy aerial opposition for the next phase. The

attempt failed because the Royal Air Force had foreseen the possibility of such attack and had widely dispersed and concealed its fighter power on the ground.

(3) The four weeks from September 6 to October 5 were those of concentrated attack on London, and were primarily an attack on the emotions of the British people.

(4) For the remainder of October, a diversified attack was carried out on urban centers throughout the country. This form of attack has continued in lessening degree ever since.

Many "experts" have been debating whether or not the concentrated German attack would have succeeded had the pressure been kept on. Some people have said that the Royal Air Force was literally out on its feet when the blitz ended. Others have argued that even though this statement may contain elements of truth, the Germans withdrew for the same reason themselves, or because they could not continue to stand the losses imposed by the Hurricanes and Spitfires. All this is as it may be. Probably we shall never know all the answers. But when the whole story is boiled down, Germany's failure arose from her one vital blunder, the blunder made on the day when Hitler permitted the Junker generals to talk him into maintaining even a small degree of ground control over the air.

What the *Luftwaffe* was sent out to do primarily was to soften Britain for invasion by ground forces. The loss of 700 German aircraft in the first ten days clearly demonstrated that Hitler was prepared to pay any price for a foothold, that he proposed to pound southeastern Britain into rubble, and, knowing that she was virtually defenseless, to cross the Channel and walk ashore over the ruins. We can thank our stars that his air force was designed primarily to break open the way for the panzers. The policy had succeeded everywhere else. It failed in Britain because of the superior firepower of the Royal Air Force, small though it was, and its brave men. It happened, strange to say, because the Germans had sacrificed everything, particularly armament, to speed. The German dive-bombers with their unprotected vital spots were sitting ducks for the boys in the Hurricanes and Spitfires.

The success of the British fighters against German dive-bombers led to the second phase, concentration on airdromes. The Germans had discovered that British fighters were their masters in the skies and that the only way to cope with them then was to destroy them on the ground. Fortunately Britain had plenty of airfields in its forward area and moved its chessmen about the board with such rapidity that the Germans were unable to keep up with their movement. Between decentralization and camouflage, the Germans simply couldn't find the fighters on the ground. During the second phase they lost approximately 600 aircraft, the British less than 120.

By then Goering knew only too well that the hope of softening up England for easy invasion was out of the question. The *Luftwaffe* simply could not gain control of Britain's air. By then they were even having difficulty in maintaining control of their own air over the occupied countries across the English Channel.

The third and fourth phases of the blitz, then, were phases which had never entered into German pre-blitz calculations. When the Germans turned on London and sought to destroy it, they were going back to a concept of warfare which has existed since the beginning of time—the idea of destroying the enemy's capital, an archaic notion. Even if Goering's air force had pounded London into a heap of unrecognizable dust, no major effect would have been felt on the outcome of the war because, thanks to modern communication systems, governments can govern from anywhere today. Thus the effect of the mass bombing of London, rather than being of advantage to Germany, merely served to kindle to white heat the anger of the people throughout the civilized world.

By the same token a great many people have misinterpreted our bombing of Berlin, choosing to see it as well-merited revenge for the London blitz. God knows revenge was merited. But you may be sure that what the United States airmen and the R.A.F. were after were aircraft factories, railway marshaling yards and terminals, the places which have to do with war production and transportation. All other demolition you can charge off to propinquity to military targets or to human error. There never was a day when one blockbuster dropped directly upon a U-boat lair at Lorient was not of infinitely greater value to the Allied cause than the wiping out of all the government office buildings in the whole German capital. That kind of bombing merely relates the airplane to the warfare of the days of Napoleon, and military aviation will never function in the atmosphere of Waterloo.

Germany lost the third phase. Her casualties in aircraft were tremendous, Britain's infinitesimal by comparison. On one day alone, September 15, 1940, 185 German aircraft were brought down on the English soil. During the blitz the Germans lost 2375 airplanes in England in daylight alone. How many were lost in the night raids, by plunging into the sea, or by crashing on the way home, nobody knows.

Germany lost the Battle of Britain because the Fuehrer allowed himself to be led aside from the real purposes of combat aviation by old men who still thought in terms of war on the ground. He compromised—and lost his one big chance.

The inertia, the timidity, and, above all, the jealousy of old-fashioned military and naval leaders on our side prevented us from taking the fullest possible advantage of Germany's failure. Our airmen had been able to enforce their determination to acquire the types of aircraft most needed—the highly armed, well-protected fighter and the well-armored and well-armed bomber which sacrificed speed to its own protection, and its bomb-load. Our aircraft were superior to any the Germans could marshal against us. What nearly cost us our life was that we did not have them in sufficient quantity. During what may be called the Munich period, when the Chamberlain Government toyed gingerly with rearmament, the Royal Air Force came into possession of a few machines of the latest types, and they were the best in the sky. But the politicians continued to relate national salvation to dollars and cents. Thus, with the thunderheads of war on the point of collision in the sky over Europe, the Royal Air Force still could not extract enough money to arm itself properly. No men who have ever lived in the civilized world will ever merit greater gratitude from the people of that world than the handful of aviation scientists who gave us the Spitfire and the Hurricane and the bomber types in use in 1940 and 1941.

Germany, of course, had gone all-out on aircraft production. Barred from becoming a major naval power, she had taken to the air. She had kicked over all the traditional traces in the military sense and had broken into the clear, aerially speaking. But for the continuing influence of old-line Navy and Army men on Hitler, Germany might have given us an air war which no nation or combination of nations could have withstood. Fortunately she didn't. We ought to decorate those old Junkers, as a mark of our eternal gratitude and their stupidity, a stupidity only equaled by that of our own old-line warriors. Rather, it would be more sensible to reflect on the possibility that some day an aggressor nation will turn everything loose in the air and destroy any enemy which has failed to keep pace in the realm of development, either qualitatively or quantitatively.

You may be sure the Germans learned their lesson in the Battle of Britain, learned that the zenith of an air war consists in bringing to bear on the enemy a force which will eliminate that enemy's own air-power. At last we followed this course in our descent upon Europe. We never made Germany's mistake, thanks to our designers and to the men responsible for Royal Air Force direction, of under-arming our aircraft. What is more, we profited from the experience gained in the Battle of Britain and learned, largely from the mistakes of our enemies, the tremendous striking power of the airplane and how best it may be used.

CHAPTER 2

Wings Over the Oceans

BEFORE much more than a year of World War II had passed, airmen operating from Canada had completely subjugated the treacherous North Atlantic and laid the foundations of a network of global airways which are the first line of communication of the United Nations today.

The story of the establishment of the first transocean bomber ferry is one of the strangest tales to come out of the war years. It was born of the womb of our necessity and peril. It played a great role in saving Britain, and, therefore, our Western civilization.

When the British nations and France declared war on Germany, Britain was starving for aircraft—particularly planes for Coastal Command patrols and for attacking the enemy's installations. At first it was impossible to secure machines from the United States, the only possible source of supply, because Uncle Sam in 1939 was doing no business with *any* belligerent. Soon, however, Washington, thanks to President Roosevelt, relented sufficiently to establish the cash-on-the-barrelhead policy, under which all belligerent nations were at liberty to purchase war materials in the United States, provided they paid the bills and took delivery at dockside in America, or at the border. Hence Britain could acquire essential aircraft as long as her money held out, for she had no problem in taking delivery. While Germany technically enjoyed the same privilege, she had no means of sending for supplies, for the British and Canadian Navies saw to it that her ships reached no American ports. Britain was ready to pay any price for aircraft in 1940. Over the seas the Royal Air Force was operating what it called "Scarecrow Patrols"—utilizing aircraft of any kind it could put into the air, including Elementary Trainers, even machines borrowed from the Sunday flying-clubs, to creep slowly up and down over the approaches to the harbors of the United Kingdom and keep the U-boats down. The call, then, was for aircraft, aircraft, aircraft, any kind of aircraft, at any price the manufacturers and owners wanted to put on their product.

Next came the problem of delivery. To send planes to Britain by sea according to methods dictated by the necessary practices of the "Sea Age" involved dismantling, crating, a long sea voyage, uncrating, reassembly in Britain, adjustment, and testing. Hence months elapsed between the time of a machine's departure from its American assembly line and its arrival in the air of Europe, ready for combat. The rate of loss at sea was extremely heavy, too, for those were the days of our greatest shipping losses in the North Atlantic.

While the Battle of Britain was at its height, a group of Canadian businessmen met in a Montreal hotel. They had been brought together by the late Sir Edward Beatty, president of the Canadian Pacific Railway, then acting in North America in the British Government's behalf in relation to the co-ordination of merchant shipping. Those present included Morris Wilson, president of the Royal Bank of Canada, and Harold Long, a hard-driving young man who in times of peace had represented the British steel industry in the Dominion.

Sir Edward told the group the dire emergency of Britain's aircraft problem. He believed that a plan to fly medium-range bombers across the Atlantic was feasible, no matter what the experts had said only a few months before, and that aircraft could be delivered with an infinitely smaller margin of loss by air, as well as with a far greater saving of time, than when sent forward by water. Those present agreed. Anything which would help Britain to stick it out was worth trying. The British, for their part, said that even if they faced a loss of 10 per cent, getting the other 90 per cent through would justify it. By the time the meeting ended the nucleus of the non-profit organization soon to be known as Atfero—Atlantic Ferry Organization—had been formed, and its members had decided to negotiate a test purchase of fifty Hudsons, to assemble air crews to fly them across the Atlantic, and to judge what the future of their operation should be by the results of first experiment. In the beginning they functioned through Canadian Pacific air service, but soon assumed independent status.

The first job was to acquire a Canadian operational base and a jump-off field in Newfoundland. This was easily solved by acquiring privileges at St. Hubert Field in Montreal. After hurried survey of the terrain, it was decided to take over an area of level ground in the hinterland of Newfoundland at what was then called Hattie's Camp and which is now the great Gander transoceanic airdrome. Runways were constructed in a hurry. Four or five old railway cars were moved to the site to provide an operations room, radio quarters, weather bureau, offices and barracks. The C.P.R. loaned the services of its top-ranking aviation executive, former ace Canadian bush-pilot, Captain C. H. (Punch) Dickins, who assembled crews and directed them. Dickins delved into the ranks of the Canadian bush-pilots, offered his old friends jobs as "aerial truck drivers," and impressed many of them into his service. Old-time Canadian fliers and a number of American airline pilots of adventurous instinct hurried to Montreal and signed articles to fly the ocean.

Meanwhile, the question of how deliveries were to be taken posed a serious problem. The terms of cash-and-carry insisted that the purchaser take delivery at the American border or seaboard. Therefore American pilots were not permitted by their own country to fly across the border to deliver the planes at Canadian airdromes, but must come to earth on the right side of their own boundary. Similarly, the Canadians were not at liberty to cross into the United States and take delivery of aircraft direct from the manufacturer on his own field. The solution was amazing and fantastic. American pilots put their wheels down literally within inches of the Canadian border. Almost within hand-clasping distance, but on the other side of the Imaginary Line, the Canadian crews who would fly the aircraft away waited. Ropes were thrown across the boundary by the Canadians and attached to the aircraft by the Americans on the neutral side. Then tractors, or horses, sometimes even oxen, stationed on the Canadian side of the border, pulled on the ropes and towed the aircraft across into Canadian territory. To think that such things can happen between such good neighbors is almost beyond imagination. Yet so choosy had we become in our interpretation of what makes one nation belligerent and the other nonbelligerent, so strong was Isolationist influence in the United States, that to observe the letter of a regulation came to mean more than to preserve the spirit of our friendship. The important point, however, was that Britain got its aircraft in time to launch them into the air against the Nazis.

The first fifty Hudsons reached Newfoundland via the strange border-crossing method late in the autumn of 1940. In the meantime a handful of Air Force officers and men, including Air Vice-Marshal D. C. T. Bennett, D.S.O., who had been captured in and escaped from Norway and later organized the R.A.F.'s Pathfinder Squadrons, which light the bombers' targets in Fortress Europe, had been sent to Canada from Britain.

The first flight of seven Hudsons left Newfoundland, led by Bennett during the night of November 10–11, 1940, and landed at Aldergrove, Northern Ireland, without the loss of a plane or man, after a crossing of little more than ten hours. The time of delivery of aircraft from American factories to the war front in Britain had been cut from, say four months, to a matter of days, making allowance for weather and other delays. What seems almost more important is that the businessmen responsible for this revolutionary event had themselves stepped unconsciously from the flat map world of the Sea Age across the threshold of the Air Age. Gone were the time-lagging, cumbersome tasks of dismantling, crating, loading, shipping, unloading, uncrating, reassembling, adjusting, and retesting. Now the aircraft were self-delivered over the ocean. With dire extremity staring them in the eyes, free men were waking up at last!

Everywhere our awakening had been delayed until we walked along the rim of the precipice of disaster. Throughout the months of what the press called "the phony war," even Britain had failed to speed war production toward its peak despite the fact that our alibi for Munich had been that it gave us time to arm. During those months the morale of the British people had decreased instead of working toward fever pitch. Then came Dunkirk; after it the Blitz of Britain—and Britain woke up, was galvanized into life by the brave words of Winston Churchill. Seldom, if ever, has there been such a response to the clarion call to arms. Britain stood ready to fight on the beaches, in the streets—with shovels, pikestaffs, anything a man could take in his hands. In the factories the people toiled endless hours to make the tools of war. The women of Britain turned their faces to the foe, to the tasks of production, with the same dauntless courage which imbued their men. They were citizens first, women second, a phenomenon not often witnessed by mortal man! This indeed was Britain's shining hour.

Canada, too, had been asleep, moving toward the war production peak as if time were on our side, as if we were planning a normal business campaign, not a war for survival. Our people and press still thought of the words "war" and "trenches" as if they were synonymous. The truth of the matter is that none of us, even in the British Commonwealth of Nations, went to war at all until Dunkirk at last taught us the implications of Nazi aggression.

So too with the United States, where only a few leaders recognized the full weight of the evidence even after Dunkirk. Most Americans still believed themselves safe behind their ocean barriers. Many were still convinced that the war beyond the Atlantic remained European in its context. Some even believed that Uncle Sam "could do business with Hitler." Not so President Roosevelt. Mr. Roosevelt knew the score and was determined to do everything in his power to halt Hitler at the Biscay coast. But in a democracy leaders can move no faster than their people—else the people will jettison the leaders and choose new men pledged to the people's views. Thus we saw the step-by-step movement through cash-on-the-barrelhead to Lend-Lease to the convoying of merchantmen in the West Atlantic, until finally the issue was joined in the smoking ruins of Pearl Harbor.

I can remember how impatient the man on the street in Canada used to feel about his well-beloved neighbors as he stood by and watched their step-by-step progress from Peace to War. But I realize now that our impatience was born of watching our friends making the identical mistakes we had made, awakening to the implications of the hour as we had awakened. As with us, what was required was a Dunkirk. And Pearl Harbor was America's Dunkirk. But about the ferry experiment—

When those fifty Hudsons reached Britain in safety and in the order of their departure from Newfoundland, piloted by their pick-up Canadian and American captains, a new era opened in transoceanic flight. The provision of navigating officers presented no problem, as the R.A.F. supplied them from its Coastal Command in Britain. To find radio operators had been extremely difficult, however. The problem was solved through the medium of radio broadcasts in which Atfero, without indicating the purpose for which men were needed, simply asked experienced operators to communicate at once with the station to which they were listening with a view to accepting special work of an extremely secret nature. They turned up from all over North America, one young man checking in from Aklavik, where the MacKenzie River empties into the Arctic Ocean in Canada's Northwest Territories.

After the experimental period, Atfero was taken under the wing of Lord Beaverbrook, then Britain's Minister of Aircraft Production. Britain's need for aircraft grew constantly more desperate. To find air crews was by no means easy, for the standards established were extremely high. A pilot seeking to join must prove at least 750 hours on twin-engined aircraft, including full knowledge of and experience in instrument flying, and must carry a commercial ticket. No search for pilots was necessary, however, for the aviation grapevine is the greatest news agency in the world. Experienced men reported from all over the continent to Montreal's St. Hubert Airport, used as temporary headquarters while the huge Dorval Field was in the course of construction. Of those who were taken on at the beginning, every survivor was still in the service in 1944.

Atfero continued until July 1941, by which time its pilots not merely flew the North Atlantic but were delivering Catalina flying boats to Britain via Bermuda.

Suddenly the American public awakened to the fact that aircraft of United States manufacture were in use overseas when it was reported that the German battleship *Bismarck*, sent to the bottom of the Atlantic by the Royal Navy, had been spotted by a Catalina serving with the British. Isolationists immediately began to ask questions. Some of the more extreme gentlemen wanted the whole business stopped at once. Questions of delivery methods were raised. Finally President Roosevelt announced his intention of "regularizing" the procedure. As a first step the American Commander-in-Chief established the United States Army Air Corps Ferry Command, the primary purpose of which would be to deliver American-built bombers to Montreal, and thereby be rid of the cross-border tow-line burlesque. The United States Army Air Corps, which would make all future deliveries, expressed a wish to hand over U. S. built aircraft to a military organization in Canada, however, whereas Atfero was a purely civilian set-up. In mid-'41, therefore, the Atlantic ferry service was turned over by its organizers to the Royal Air Force Ferry Command under Air Chief Marshal Sir Frederick Bowhill, with heaaquarters in Montreal. The major portion of its pilots, however, remained civilian, at one time almost 90 per cent of the ferry captains being American. The United States agreed at the time of the "militarization" of the service to make no claim for the return of such personnel in the event that the United States should go to war. The service expanded with tremendous rapidity.

At the time of Pearl Harbor and during the first few months of American participation in the war, its personnel were able to solve many riddles of delivery for an unprepared Uncle Sam. By the spring of 1944, as the Royal Air Force Transport Command, Atlantic Group, it counted amongst its air crew fliers of seventeen nationalities to a four-figure total in numbers.

The world-wide network of military airways which today carry the fliers of the United Nations to every point of the compass, to every continent, across the top of the world to Russia, across the deserts of Africa and the jungles of Burma, had its origin, then, in the meeting of a group of Canadian civilians in a Montreal hotel. The fliers of this service pioneered the Pacific to Australia and made the first aircraft deliveries to General MacArthur before the American Government was ready to take over its own transpacific ferrying tasks. They opened routes across the Arctic and sub-Arctic, over the stepping stones to Britain through Labrador, Greenland, and Iceland. They pioneered the South Atlantic route through Belen and Natal, Brazil; to the Gold Coast by way of Ascension Island. Thus by the spring of 1943 the Atlantic Ferry had become a global organization. From Montreal deliveries of Canadian and American aircraft were being made to Britain, Southeast Asia, North Africa, India, to almost any point on the map of the world. From Montreal, American-built Liberators have made the longest non-stop flights in aviation history. The Command operates its own shuttle service to bring crews back to Canada in a hurry for new transocean flights. As the pioneer of the world-wide ferry system, it has made one of the greatest contributions to global aviation in the history of flight.

Every aircraft moving forward from North America to a war zone serves a triple purpose:

(1) It is a new weapon.

(2) It carries a load of emergent freight to the scene of hostilities.

(3) It fills up its empty spaces with new air crew graduates, conveying them to the scene of action with less time lag than obtains under any other method of transportation.

The Ferry also carries Government-sponsored passengers between Washington, Ottawa, and London. It has been widely used to smash mail bottlenecks and cheerfully boasts that it is the greatest mail-carrier in the world. During 1943 alone its aircraft delivered 15,000,000 pieces of mail to troops overseas.

Long before the United Nations' invasion of the European continent the R.A.F. Transport Command was sharing its bases with the United States Army Air Corps interchangeably, and flying bombers to the theaters of war for the United States Army as and when Uncle Sam was hard-pressed for air crews. More than 12,000 Atlantic crossings had been made by the spring of 1944, and less than forty aircraft lost. In other words, the rate of loss was less than three aircraft in every thousand flown over the oceans, whereas there were times when losses of planes shipped by sea reached desperate percentages.

The global airway network of the United Nations was established under circumstances infinitely more difficult than those which would have obtained under conditions of peace. Under normal circumstances of flight weather reports would be available from hour to hour and minute to minute from ships all over the oceans of the world. In total war ships maintain radio silence and so are not available as sources of information. Thus the weather experts of the over-ocean airways were forced to find new ways of prophesying what lay ahead for the aviator who was about to jump off across the North Atlantic, or any other major over-water gap. They did so. Meteorological knowledge increased during four years of war more than in the previous thirty. So, too, with every factor of long-range flight. The circumstances of war and its emergent necessities have taught us lessons we might never have learned under the ambling conditions of peace.

At the time of this writing the United Nations are involved as partners in a world-wide airway network. We have not all gone about the job in the same way. Each country has its own manner of doing things, its own idiosyncrasies, and its own pet schemes. But all have worked together in closest harmony, with complete exchange of facilities and information and no secrets between partners. We have also achieved, at long last, an operational unity between land, sea, and air forces which has been a decisive factor in turning the tide of battle. If only we could have reached these two profoundly essential goals years ago, how different the story of the early stages of World War II might have been. Together they create an indispensable state of affairs which must persist in the days of peace if we are to enjoy the full benefits of the Air Age and avoid its potential curse.

C H A P T E R 3

The Making of a Combat Flier

THERE is no better example of the impact of the Air Age upon a people than the story of aviation in Canada. It was from Canada's soil that the first flight in the British Empire took place. By the end of World War I almost 25 per cent of the flying personnel of the Royal Air Force were young Canadians. Between the two wars, Canadians were the pioneers in the use of aviation as a means of breaking open the frontiers. With the coming of World War II it was in Canada, under Canadian direction, that the nucleus of today's network of global military airways took shape. To Canada, too, belongs the honor of having brought into being the air-training plan which has become the pattern on which those of all the United Nations are founded and which became largely responsible for the Allies' superiority in the air both in their own and the enemies' sky during the final phases of the war. When peace returns, Canada will play again an all-out role in the Air Age, for she stands at the crossroads of the world's aerial highways and at the dead center of the new heartland of air geography.

In World War II, as in World War I, young Canadians rushed into the air to play again far more than an ordinary role against the enemies of freedom. As this is written they are fighting in their tens of thousands all over the world. The 100,000th Canada-trained flying man has won his wings, a figure comparable to 1,500,000 American fliers in ratio to population.

When the Canadian people went to war against Germany in September 1939, most people thought in terms of a replica of World War I: a war of blockade and attrition in which the Royal Navy would prevent supplies reaching Germany while the armies of the Allies resumed the trench warfare aspect of World War I under the somewhat more commodious and certainly more sanitary conditions of the Maginot Line. In those early weeks all that Canada heard was Army, Army, Army. Critics of the Government, in Parliament, in the Press, and at public dinners and rallies were constantly wanting to know when the Army would be equipped and ready to move into the mud of Flanders. Not until well into October was any talk heard about the air. Apparently the overrunning of Poland by the *Luftwaffe* had made as little impression on the Canadian people as on those of the United States, France, or Britain.

The news of the great Air Plan came with dramatic suddenness on October 10, 1939, when the Prime Minister announced in Ottawa that the Governments of Britain, Australia, New Zealand, and Canada had decided to undertake a great mutual scheme, the setting for which would be the North American Dominion. Weeks passed while the scheme was being hammered into shape and on December 17 the complete plan was given to the world. All that it needed to make it tick was aircraft for its candidates to fly and equipment for them to wear, for the youngsters themselves were banging on the doors of the recruiting offices in thousands, demanding to be let in.

Tribute must be paid here to those who laid the ground work for this plan months before Germany invaded Poland. It was largely due to the untiring efforts of the Honorable Ian Mackenzie, then Minister of Defense, that the program had progressed so far by the time war was declared, and to his successor, the Honorable Norman Rogers, later killed in an aircraft accident, that it was so successfully put into effect so soon after the outbreak of war.

It was an ambitious scheme, as aviation plans looked in 1939. Canada undertook to create a vast chain of training fields from coast to coast, approximately sixty in number, plus the necessary ground establishments. Britain would provide the bulk of the training aircraft. Trainees would include not only pilots but observers and wireless-air gunners, men who would be both radio operators and gunners.

Before the plan could get into its stride, however, France fell, Dunkirk happened, and the British countries stood alone. As the thunderbolts of aerial blitzkrieg rained down on Britain, the temptation for Canada was to rush overseas all capable flying personnel, men trained as instructors under the plan to help stem the tide of the *Luftwaffe*. The temptation would have been easy to follow. In fact, if Canadians had accepted the viewpoint of large sections of the press of the United States at the time they would have thrown their available human material into the pot and washed their hands of the whole business, for those were the days when many of Canada's American neighbors expected that the British Commonwealth, standing alone as it did against the German horde, must soon capitulate.

To add to the problems of the organizers and administrators of the plan, word came through from Britain that no training aircraft as called for in the plan would be available from Britain. Actually ships on the high seas carrying planes to Canada were turned back in mid-ocean. The Canadian Government and its dynamic Air Minister, the Honorable C. G. Power, and his senior officers promptly confounded the defeatists by announcing that they would double the scope and output of the plan, a quixotic decision, perhaps, but one which has been responsible in great degree for the R.A.F.'s successes in the air, inasmuch as it has provided a great part of the trained air crews. Members of the Ministry of Munitions and Supply, including the Minister, the Honorable C. D. Howe, worked day and night to gear Canada's domestic aircraft industry to the production of Elementary and Service Trainers. Almost insuperable was the task of finding engines, for Canada had no engine industry. Mr. Howe found a source of supply in the United States. At last a trickle of aircraft began to come through. Meanwhile the Canadian construction industry was tearing the countryside apart and creating huge airdromes and essential buildings. The number of projected fields was almost doubled. Classes were recruited and started ground training in the hope that by the time they were ready to fly at least a few training aircraft would be available. The help of the civilian flying clubs and their equipment was impressed into service. Somehow, by guess and by God, the machinery began to roll.

By the end of 1940 more than half of the projected Elementary Flying Training Schools had been opened. During 1941 all were running in high gear. Now and then classes were delayed between the Elementary and Service training stages, waiting for fields to be ready or equipment to be delivered. Yet by the middle of 1941 the plan was in full production at almost double its original concept. Boys from all the British countries were in training in Canada. Thousands already had arrived in the theaters of war. Young Americans appeared in great numbers at the Canadian Recruiting Offices begging for a crack at the Nazis. An "unofficial" recruiting committee headed by Group Captain Homer Smith of Toronto and New

York and Clayton Knight, the well-known illustrator, both veterans of the Royal Air Force of World War I, was established in New York and acted as an "underground railway" through which thousands of American youngsters made their way to Canada to join the Royal Canadian Air Force. If there were those who criticized the proceedings, and there were many American isolationists who did so, the work of the Clayton Knight committee paid off a thousandfold after Pearl Harbor. For from the ranks of the R.C.A.F., Uncle Sam was able to draw off almost 2000 trained American fliers into his own service, youngsters immediately available for urgent duties in their own country's hour of need.

The British Commonwealth Air Training Plan is the cornerstone on which the British Empire's vast air-power has been built. It stands today as the pattern for all, including the United States itself, in the realm of mass production of combat fliers.

Attention has been paid in an earlier chapter to the manner in which youngsters were accepted for air crew service in the first war in the air, and a hit-and-miss business it was, the result of which was that the average pilot picked up most of his knowledge of combat aviation under fire. Twenty hours in the air was as much as the pupil could reasonably expect before he joined issue with the enemy. In other words, most of us learned to fly in combat, and if you could survive the first month with the help of your experienced mates, you were doing well. A comparison then-and-now brings out again the revolution which has extended into the realm of training for war flying, just as it has extended into every corner of the world of flight.

The young man who is admitted into the sacred precincts of the air training school of today is no haphazard selection but one of the cream of the crop of this generation of fighting men. The medical examinations and re-examinations to which he is subjected leave no loophole through which the physically imperfect youngster can hope to escape into the air. Either he is the 100 per cent perfect physical specimen or he remains groundbound for life so far as our Air Forces are concerned. He is subjected to all manner of tests in decompression chambers where his reactions to power dives, pull-outs, and sharp climbs and his responses to various atmospheric conditions, with and without the aid of oxygen, are recorded. If he inclines to be air-sick he soon finds himself back on the ground. Only the sound and the strong reach the Wings Parade.

The electro-cardiograph tests the young man's heart, and electro-encephalography records the reactions of his brain. In the realm of air medicine Canada has been the world's teacher, for it was in Canada's Banting Institute, headed by the late, great Sir Frederick Banting, that modern methods of weeding out the unfit-to-fly were largely developed.

Under the Canadian training system, the trainee goes through a ground school period of at least three months before he leaves the ground. If he is successful in his examinations he then reports to Elementary Flying Training School. Here his working hours are divided almost evenly into classroom work and flying, the standard equipment being the Fairchild Cornell, now manufactured in the Dominion in huge quantities. The pupil is broken-in much less harshly than was the case in World War I. First, he has spent many hours "flying" the Link trainer on the ground. Thus by the time he takes to the air, he knows many of the answers and proceeds to apply them to actual flight. Finally he solos after considerable more dual instruction than the old-timers ever had. Then comes a period of twenty hours' solo, at the end of which he is given his first flying examination by his instructor. To go on he must show great promise. If he is ham-fisted or "slow in the mental uptake" he will be changed to one of the several other air crew categories or, if considered hopeless, will be allotted to one of seventy-two ground trades. Successful, he carries on with more elementary flying. At the fifty-hour mark he is put through an extremely stiff flying examination. If he makes the grade he moves on from aviation's high school into its university, Service Flying Training School. By this time his instructors will have decided to what branch of aviation he should go, whether he should become a fighter pilot or fly as one of a bomber crew. If he is what may be called the steady type, bombers are his likely destination. If he is a happy-go-lucky, devil-may-care youngster, he has the makings of a fighter pilot. There are no hard and fast rules, but these are generally applicable definitions.

At Service School the pupil immediately finds himself back to dual control and living under the watchful eye of an instructor. Soon he is off again solo. Long weeks of all-hours flying follow. No longer does inclement weather keep him groundbound. When he has nothing else to do he practices aerobatics, learns to land his machine under every imaginable condition. He practices all manner of trick take-offs. He must pass the most difficult navigation tests. He learns how to fly in formation as a member of a closely knit team, for this is a teamwork flying war, whereas the first war in the air was very largely individual. At the end of approximately ten weeks he marches out on parade with his fellows and receives his coveted wings.

But still the young man is only beginning. Next comes Operational Training, during which he is schooled on the types of machines he will fly in actual combat. If he is destined to be a fighter pilot he will fly single-seaters and learn all the tricks of the trade under conditions identical with those of actual combat, conditions which lack only the spatter of enemy bullets or the crump of bursting ack-ack. He dogfights all over the sky with his fellow-pupils. If he is to be a bomber pilot, or a member of a bomber crew, he must be schooled to become a cog in the machine that is the ship's company of a Lancaster, Wellington, Fortress, or Liberator. It is a teamwork job, first, last, and always.

Thus by the time today's young aviator is ready for war he is the completely schooled flier, a man who knows every trick of the trade and has no lessons to learn in battle, other than those which inescapably cannot be learned anywhere else. A vast gap separates flying training as we knew it in World War I and the methods in use today. It could not be otherwise. It is, in fact, just one additional mark of the revolution which has taken place all over the skies. Aviation is no longer a hit-and-miss business, but one of the world's most skilled trades. In 1916 if a man could fly one type of aircraft it was assumed that after an hour or two of practice he could fly any other type. That view ceased to be valid long ago. You cannot pull a man out of the cockpit of a Cornell trainer this afternoon and drop him into the office of a Spitfire, pat him on the back, and send him off to look for the enemy and expect him to come back alive, because the Spitfire would probably polish him off long before he encountered his first enemy plane. The value of the human being and his life has been the primary consideration of the democratic nations. Hence our training for combat in this war has always been much more complete than that employed by our enemies, neither of whom has ever given even passing thought to the importance of human life, as such. Their aircraft have always sacrificed the safety of the crew to speed. Their training cannot even be compared to that of the United States or the British Nations. Such factors as these are in large degree responsible for the British victory in the Battle of Britain and for American superiority in the Pacific and in mass-raids over the Reich. Give our lads the machines to fly and no question remains as to who's who in the air—a far cry from the position in which we found ourselves in Britain in 1940, or which obtained in the Pacific immediately after Pearl Harbor.

CHAPTER 4

The Free World Hits Back

ON JUNE 6, 1944, the armed forces of the Western Democracies landed on the beaches of Normandy to set in motion on the ground what had been proceeding in the skies for many weeks —the greatest battle for human liberation in man's history. D-Day, the day of which men in countries enslaved and in countries still free had spoken almost in awe, ever since the appalling hour of Dunkirk, had dawned at last. Free men had returned to the soil of France to set France free from the Nazi yoke.

The invasion of France and the establishment of the Normandy beachhead would have been impossible without control of the air on D-Day, or for that matter without a preceding invasion—the invasion of metropolitan France, which was intrinsically an invasion by air. The huge armada of 4000 ships that steamed boldly across the English Channel, and as boldly loosed men in tens of thousands and matériel in thousands of tons against Germany's vaunted Atlantic Wall, was able to do so with only minor molestation solely because of the democracies' air-power. The air belonged to us. The *Luftwaffe* did not even choose to argue the point.

But the blow struck on D-Day was not the initial fact of the invasion. For months on end our bombers had blasted Germany's heavy industries, the major factory areas of enslaved France, key railways and roads, marshaling yards, junction points, enemy installations of every sort. This was the softening-up process. It was a process which not merely brought havoc to German war production but seriously impeded the movement of men and arms into the forward defense zones. Raids involving heavy bombers in four-figure force were so much the routine of preparation as to become almost dull commonplace to the newspaper reader (though not, I venture to think, to the victims).

Next the air forces of the United States and the British Commonwealth turned their attention to the Invasion Coast. For an extended period they rained bombs in thousand-ton lots on Hitler's vaunted coastal defenses. Long before the first infantry and the first tanks swarmed over the dunes, massed-aircraft attacks had pounded the so-called impregnable works of the great German engineer, Todt, into rubble. Our troops were able to secure their first footholds without serious resistance because the bombers had first breached the walls of the fortress, because our fighters swept the skies clear of the *Luftwaffe* to open the way for the landing of groundborne forces, and because of the landing of airborne troops in force behind the enemy's lines.

Actually Germany had built its own Maginot Line along the Channel Coast and then proceeded to fall prey to the same stupid assumption which had resulted in the military downfall of France in 1940—the assumption that a ground fortress could be made impregnable in the Air Age. In 1940 Germany had assumed, and correctly, that ground fortifications as a sole means of defense are useless, for the excellent reason that the young man in an airplane refuses to recognize that they are there and simply leap-frogs them. Yet four years later Germany herself became the victim of what had previously been her own concept of modern attack. She rested her case on the coastal Maginot of Normandy, left it virtually undefended from the air, and so lost this phase of the battle.

On D-Day the Western Democracies threw no less than 11,000 aircraft against the enemy. The skies over the Channel were black with Fortresses, Lancasters, Liberators, Wellingtons and Halifaxes, shuttling between Britain and the ground-invasion area to dump their loads of death and destruction on the enemy. British Mosquitoes harassed his communications. Rocket-firing Beaufighters and Typhoons, Hurricane bombers and Hotspurs strafed the rear areas. The new clipped-wing Spitfires poured lead into the enemy from tree-top height, took close-up pictures of every phase of the ground action as it developed.

Uncle Sam's bombers were escorted by Thunderbolts, with high-flying Mustangs cruising along the roof, looking for German fighters. Every efficient aircraft type seen on the fighting fronts of 1943 and 1944 was present *en masse* that day. The United Nations owned the air.

As the armada of naval and merchant ships, all manner of barges and carriers, rode a choppy Channel, great fleets of aircraft passed overhead on a special aerial mission. They carried paratroopers and gliderborne soldiers—*the men who were the first wave of the ground attack.* Crossing the coast, the troop-carriers flew well inland before releasing thousands of parachutists over strategic crossroads, bridgeheads, and fortifications. Behind them came the gliders, including Britain's huge new Hamilcar, a veritable flying boxcar, more than 100 feet in wingspread. The Hamilcar can be glided into a small meadow at half the landing speed of any engined aircraft. Once aground, its fuselage is lowered to grasstop level and a door in its nose falls forward and becomes a landing ramp, down which rolls a reconnaissance tank, ready for battle. Thus did the first wave of the ground invasion sweep onto the soil of France—from the air! The task committed to those who flew in and landed behind the German lines was that of harassing and confusing the enemy, of blowing up vital bridges and other communications, of silencing guns, of preventing the Germans from organizing counter-blows the result of which might have been to throw the amphibious operation back into the sea. For three days Allied airborne troops so harassed the enemy in the rear, infiltrated so deeply into his own support areas, that the German staff was unable to deliver any counterattack of major proportions. In short, airborne troops made possible the landings in force of those who came by sea to the beachheads.

In the light of such evidence, then, can anyone doubt for a moment that air-power was the prime factor in the act of invasion, from the beginnings of the softening-up program to the moment of landing in France? Once more superiority in the air had brought superiority to every other arm. First came the long process of softening-up, of delivering a series of round-the-clock hammer blows on German industry and communications from the air. Next came the blasting of the Invasion Coast. Finally came the first landings in Normandy, made from the air. All these things happened before a single infantryman or a single shipborne tank reached the beaches. Certainly this is not said to minimize in the slightest degree the heroism of those who came to Normandy by sea, nor to belittle the skill with which the ground forces launched their attack. It is said to emphasize the tremendous impact of Allied air-power in France and elsewhere behind the German lines and to drive home that success again attended those who went into battle in possession of control of the air. Never in the history of combat aviation have such blows been struck as those which came from the 11,000 aircraft which fought on D-Day!

What had happened between the desperate autumn of 1939 and the triumphal dawn of June 6, 1944, to make the events of that history-making day possible?

First, the airplane had become infinitely more lethal in 1944 than it was when Germany invaded Poland—more lethal in its own striking power against ground or seaborne forces, more lethal in the weapons it was able to mount for combat with other aircraft.

Second, the production capacity of the world's aircraft industry has been expanded almost to infinity. Aircraft plants in the United States and the British Nations produced almost 30,000 aircraft in 1943 alone.

Third, global aviation which was in its childhood in 1939 had become a full-grown adult in 1944. Today aircraft are not merely *capable* of flying from anywhere in the world to anywhere else in the world, but are doing so constantly.

The British showed the way in the realm of aircraft armament in the years immediately previous to World War II. The sanity of the approach of Britain's designers and engineers, perhaps in even greater degree than the gallantry and never-say-die spirit of the R.A.F.'s fighter pilots, won the Battle of Britain and drove off the concentrated attack of the *Luftwaffe,* intended to spearhead Hitler's invasion. Had the Hurricanes and Spitfires of 1940 almost completely sacrificed armor and armament to speed, as the Germans had done, disaster might easily have been visited upon the British. Nobody but the British appeared to have recognized the value of fire-power up to that time. The Germans scoffed at it. To them speed was everything. They regarded the campaigns of Poland, France, Belgium, Holland, Denmark, and Norway as bearing out their belief that speed above all is the primary force of air war. They still went along with the idea of cockpit-mounted machine guns firing in synchronization with the revolutions of a propeller, which reduces the force of the guns to the speed of the propeller's rotations. They gave their rear gunners little armament and they virtually deprived bomber crews, from cockpit to tail, of defensive armor.

Britain on the other hand loaded up the wings of her fighters with hard-hitting machine guns and cannon. She gave the pilot every possible ounce of protection from the enemy's fire. She equipped her bombers, great and small, with revolving turrets and their crews with as much armament as can possibly be introduced into an airplane. And she proved that she was right by the success of her air-arm, both in defense and on the offensive.

Nobody else had the common sense to follow her example. It is not for me to criticize the prewar aviation policy of the United States, but perhaps I may be forgiven for calling attention to some of its weaknesses, for they were of such a nature that if Uncle Sam had been forced to go to war in 1939, his air-arm would have been as vulnerable as the *Luftwaffe* turned out to be under the guns of the R.A.F., and would have lacked the striking power which the German Air Force brought to bear in the subjugation of Western Europe.

The United States developed the dive-bomber. Yet Hitler showed the American Army Air Corps how to use it and the Royal Air Force demonstrated its weakness when lightly armed and armored. Almost up to the time of Pearl Harbor the United States Army was still manufacturing obsolete observation aircraft, obsolete because the day of such lumbering vehicles passed long ago. Today only the speediest fighters, capable of fighting their way through into the area of reconnaissance and battling their way home again, are of any value for observation purposes. The Americans remained strictly attached to cockpit-mounted guns as opposed to fire-power originating in the wings until long after the war began. They clung tenaciously to the idea of the propeller-synchronized machine gun. Yet at the same time America's external customers and present allies were ordering modern gun installations in the aircraft which they ordered in the United States.

So, too, with American bombers, than which no finer may be found in the world today. In the days before Pearl Harbor, the American manufacturer and designer simply could not convince his own Government of the necessity for armament and armor in the huge aircraft then being made for delivery to Uncle Sam. Fortunately for all concerned, many airplanes of all major American types went forward to Britain, first by purchase and later under Lend-Lease, and the British themselves, working under the stimulus of their life-or-death struggle, introduced many new improvements which in turn went back to the United States and were adopted there by the American forces.

The upshot of all this—and it is directly the outcome of the excellent spirit of co-operation which obtains between us as allies—is that today's American aircraft production has never been excelled in quality, and probably never equaled, anywhere in the world.

At last, throughout the world, even the most groundbound military men have come to realize that the airplane is a weapon in itself and to acknowledge that the quality of one's weapons is not of itself enough. With quality must go quantity, if the enemy is to be overwhelmed and driven from the skies. The United Nations, and in particular the United States with its mass-production mind, have demonstrated during the course of the war that it is possible to turn out the combat airplane, whether bomber or fighter, with the same assembly-line speed, standardization, and precision which obtain in the automotive industry.

Thus the United Nations found themselves at the beginning of the fifth summer of war in possession of aerial supremacy in every theater of action. They had beaten the enemy in the race of production. From the air they had not merely leap-frogged and destroyed his ground fortifications; in many areas they had virtually driven his aircraft from the skies. Beyond this they had struck crushing blows at those air forces in their places of origin, the factories and assembly lines of the Reich. After five years of war the nations ranged against Germany and Japan possessed a weapon capable of undertaking and successfully carrying out the identical mission which had sent the *Luftwaffe* over the borders of Poland in 1939—world conquest. In strengthening ourselves, in gradually catching up on our enemies and finally passing them, the United Nations had fashioned a war machine equipped as no juggernaut of battle had ever been armed before, a co-ordinated fighting machine which far surpassed in quantity and in the quality of its arms that with which Hitler came within an inch of subjugating the world.

Thank God, neither our leaders nor our people have ever entertained such ambitions! Our people loathe war. The primary ambition of the fighting man in the uniform of any of these nations is to defeat the enemy and return to his home. But the fact remains, and it is a compelling fact, that the United Nations stand armed as no other force in history has been armed and that in the air alone we possess the power to demolish any enemy or potential grouping of enemies.

How are we to utilize these great forces? How are we to control them? The force with which we have struck from the air, colossal though it has been, has by no means reached the peak of its potential performance. The nightmare boundaries of human horror are still far beyond the horizons of belief. Soon mankind must come to momentous decisions in respect of his use of the air. Shall it be for peace and the fashioning of a finer way of life for all men? Or shall it be for war, for the selfish policies of the past which can only end in new wars?

CHAPTER 5

The Battleground of Tomorrow

IT HAS been said many times that World War II was a young man's war—that elderly gentlemen in their forties are no longer physically able to support the heat and burthen of the day in the hard-hitting warfare developed during modern battle. The statement holds across the whole panorama of warfare. The youngest of all our weapons, the airplane, has become our most important. Without the airplane our battleships cannot search the seas for those of the enemy. Without the airplane our ground troops are mired and helpless. Without the airplane the enemy's fortress cannot be invaded. The airplane, in sort, has become our primary weapon of destruction. It precedes the forward movement of ground forces into the enemy's territory. Forces bound to the ground tend to become more and more forces of occupation rather than forces of attack. If ever an aggressor, or an attacker, lets go with the full potential of all-out air war, nothing will be left for the soldier on the ground to do but to march across the ruin and occupy the enemy's fortress. That is the primary lesson we must learn from the role aviation has played in its second world war.

In 1914 or 1918 the destructive power of aircraft was negligible. Our bombers were capable only of hit-and-run raids, the primary result of which was psychological. Secondary qualities were those of observation, spying out an enemy's positions and reporting them to the generals behind our own lines. The Allied nations went into World War II with the assumption still in their minds that these were the functions of aircraft. France had no air force worth mentioning because she had continued to hitch her whole military theorizing to trench warfare—the Maginot Line was nothing more or less than a trench system palatially designed and magnificently equipped. And we have seen that even the best ground defenses are useless when considered by themselves in war as we know it today, for the airplane simply hops over and lands behind them.

Or, look out to sea. When did the United Nations finally wrest control of the Atlantic from the U-boat? Through 1940, 1941, and 1942 the job of keeping open the supply line from the United States and Canada, which together constituted the primary arsenal of Democracy, had to be left almost entirely to the British and Canadian Navies. The men in the destroyers and corvettes did a job than which no finer or more courageous has ever been recorded in the history of war. But they could not assert control over an ocean into which the enemy's undersea boats were operating from bases 2000 miles away from the points of attack. Only when we were able to give our convoys the advantage of an ocean-wide aerial spotting system, only when we were able to turn aircraft carriers loose in the Atlantic to spot the submarines and drive home the attack, were we able to take control of the ocean highway and say "this is ours and we intend to keep it."

This was true with equal force in the Pacific. The tremendous blows which the American Navy began to deliver in the Pacific in 1943, the beginning of the slow but inexorable push toward Tokyo, stemmed from the arrival of more and more aircraft carriers in that ocean. From the service that they rendered in protecting their own capital ships and the blows which carrier-based aircraft delivered against the Japs came the turn in the Pacific war. Had the Japanese lacked air superiority in the Pacific through the winter of 1941 and the summer of 1942, they would never have pushed south to the borders of Australia. But they had that superiority and they went where they willed while they had it.

Such is the role which aviation played as World War II reached out day by day, month by month, and year by year to increasingly broad horizons of horror. Throughout these years the airplane marched in the van of every attack, no matter who made it. Every battle of World War II up to this writing has been won by the side which possessed superior air-striking power and sovereignty of the air over the battlefield.

Indeed the history of the years from 1939 to 1944 proves that in modern warfare victory can only come to those who possess superior air-power and the knowledge and organization for its intelligent use. As to the future, if men continue to resort to arms to settle their disputes, wars will be decided entirely by air-power. In other words, the era of landbound armies and seabound ships has come to its twilight. Intensively mechanized armies may participate in future wars, but if so it will be only in the climactic sense, as forces of final subjugation and occupation. Battles may ensue upon and under the seas, but even these will be decided in the air over those same waters. The forward strides of aviation during its second world war in a quarter century and the implications of its latest developments have been such as to demonstrate that the battleground of tomorrow will be almost entirely in the skies. If we take to those skies again to settle our disputes, such havoc will result that our civilization itself will collapse under the blow. If we do not leave World War II behind us determined that never again shall man take up arms against his brother, may God help us.

All this will sound like alarmist talk to those who are still looking at the world through yesterday's eyes. We have been confronted during this century by the most serious and urgent lessons ever to face the human species and we have been confronted by them not once but twice. In what terms are men thinking today? In what terms are our economic and political leaders talking? What world do we picture beyond victory?

The world most people picture seems to be very much like the one we left behind—a world of arrant nationalism and race pride, a world of bitter trade competition and trade barriers. Many people on the North American continent are raising particular vocal hell apropos the merits and demerits of what they call the Free Enterprise system, which seems to be just another phrase to define our old-fashioned capitalist-democracy. Certainly that is not the first question which faces mankind. That first question is whether our civilization is going to survive, or man is going to destroy it, and whether it is to be saved or destroyed through the medium of capitalism or socialism, or a mixture of both, is purely secondary. What I mean is this: If we have not learned from World War II that we *dare* not fight again, because to fight will mean the annihilation of civilization itself, then what has capitalism on the one hand or conglomerate socialism on the other to do with it? What is the difference between dying of double pneumonia or in an airplane crash? Either way a man is dead and that is the first point at issue—the death or survival of human civilization.

If World War II had been delayed for a period of ten years, or perhaps only five, and the sciences associated with aerial combat had progressed during that period as they have progressed during the years of war, this would have been the war which would have ended the civilization we have erected. Fortunately for mankind, it looks as if we are to have one more chance. That is solely because both sides entered the present conflict without minds completely attuned to the new concepts of death in, and from, the skies, and still remained committed in varying degrees to other arms of warfare. But if the weapons which have already emerged from the laboratory had been available prior to 1939 and those which are on the point of what may be called useful emergence had then been in our hands, World War II would have been almost entirely an aerial war and it would have descended to horrors not dreamed of, even by those who withstood the hammer blows of the bombardments of that greatest of all wars to date.

All manner of factors and events are quoted by those who attempt to assess the hows and whys of the survival of the United Nations in 1940, 1941, and 1942. A British Admiral, Sir Percy Noble, formerly Commander-in-Chief of Britain's Western Approaches, has given the credit to the men in the destroyers and corvettes who kept the Atlantic lifeline open. Others have said we were saved when Hitler failed to turn his landborne spearheads toward and across the English Channel. Other experts maintain that Germany lost the war through the delusions of grandeur, bordering on paresis, which led *der Fuehrer* to step across the borders of the Soviet Union; still others, that the fate of our enemies was decided on the December day when the Japanese bombed Pearl Harbor at Germany's instigation and Germany declared war on the United States of America. All these and many other factors have contributed to Freedom's survival.

But one outstanding battle of the war has been omitted from these calculations and that is the Battle of Britain. If Germany had succeeded in reducing Britain to rubble during the Blitz, or had so softened up England in that tremendous ordeal by air as to make successful invasion possible, then the war would have been lost. Germany would then have proceeded to demolish Russia alone and finally the United States, taking her own good time about it. Perhaps the United States would have come to its senses and jumped in at Russia's side to save the world from the new Attila and his horde. Of that I am not too sure. But of this I *am* sure; if it had not been for what may almost be called the accident of judgment which gave Britain aircraft better equipped to fight than those of Germany, and, even with this advantage, if Germany had not made fatal aerial blunders, then the war would have taken an entirely different turn after the fall of France. Britain would not have been the jumping-off place for the invasion of *Festung Europa.* Instead it would have been, at best, the first objective of the liberators. Let every man who believes in liberty thank his God for the engineers who designed and armed the Hurricanes and Spitfires, and for the boys who flew them in the Battle of Britain. Then let him give thanks for the blunders responsible for the *Luftwaffe's* failure to bring equal or stronger armament to bear upon the Royal Air Force. Otherwise we would not be in a position today to spend much time philosophizing about the reasons for our continued presence on earth as free nations.

That fact alone should be enough to convince us that we have passed across the threshold of the Air Age, and must live in a world in which, in peace or war, for weal or woe, aviation will be the touchstone of our whole way of life.

PART V

Where Do We Go from Here?

CHAPTER 1

The Future Is Here

ANYONE who recognizes the facts of life as they apply to the Air Age and the days ahead cannot fail to be amazed by the attitude of many people, even men closely associated with the production and flying of aircraft, toward questions which will face us all as soon as the shooting stops. To judge by their words, many laymen are sure that no further revolutionary changes are likely to occur in the skies and that, in fact, the multi-engined airplane is the alpha and omega of what the skies hold for mankind. Jets and rockets and suchlike they dismiss with a jeer.

Before me, as I write, is a copy of one of the leading financial journals of the United States, the aviation expert of which clearly pronounces the view that today's airplanes represent something approaching the total possibilities of science and then proceeds, with the strange abracadabra of his trade, to relate the whole business to commerce and profit, an approach which it seems to be impossible for men of finance ever to get out of their heads.

The gentleman does not consider the new forms of propulsion, now reaching far beyond the experimental stage, as worthy of even passing notice. He writes, in short, in approximately the same vein in which his fathers talked about the brothers Wright and like those "experts" who scoffed at the horseless carriage.

According to people who hold such views, and their number is legion, what has to be done about aviation as soon as the war is over is to get it back into commercial harness with all possible speed. They view such machines as the DC3 and DC4 as the epitome of flying efficiency—they said the same about the Camel and the DeHaviland at the end of World War I—and seem to spend their spare time thinking in terms of airlines up and down which such aircraft as the DC4 will roam at cruising speeds under 250 miles an hour, carrying a maximum of 42 passengers, while the smaller DC3, with its 21-passenger load, gallops up and down feeder routes to bring business to the trunk lines. All well and good. All that is wrong with such talk is that it fails to take into consideration the things that have happened since 1939, the things which are happening under our eyes today, and the amazing things which are bound to happen tomorrow.

One hears a great deal of idiotic talk, too, about intercontinental military airways. Over these airways, as we have already noted, thousands upon thousands of aircraft have been flown from the North American continent to the battlefronts of the world in Europe, Asia, Africa, and Australia, and to island fortresses in the Pacific and other oceans. Over these routes, as we have noted time and again, men charged with direction of the war, including the political leaders of the United Nations, their military and naval experts, diplomats, and nobody knows how many thousands of production men, are constantly in flight from the arsenals of freedom to the actual lands where freedom is being defended. Under the pressure of war we have not merely shipped overseas thousands upon thousands of aircraft from our production lines but have created all over the world facilities for safe passage—great bases and intermediate fields in Canada, Labrador, islands in the Northern and Southern Atlantic, in the jungles of Africa, on islands of the Pacific, and in every corner of the world where such facilities are required to ensure safe flight.

The opinion of "conservative minded" men, in aviation as well as on the outside, seems to be that the runways of these bases will grow weedy from lack of traffic and that their hangars and other buildings will soon rust and collapse. Some of the "experts" have tried to assess how many passengers per annum will want to fly from London to New York and how much they will be prepared to pay for the privilege. They tell us that there is not likely to be much doing in the realm of commercial traffic between, say, Chicago and Moscow, and they paint a gloomy picture of what lies beyond victory, simply because they cannot project their minds into the future, or are afraid to do so.

The solution of international air relationships must be completely divorced from the private profit instinct. If it is not so divorced and if we plunge into any form of traffic war as between nations, the only possible outcome is trouble for all concerned, not necessarily between the Germans and the Japanese on the one hand and the present United Nations on the other, but even between ourselves. Each country will probably operate its own internal and local aviation through the medium of private commerce, or by any other means it chooses. That is for each nation to decide according to its own whims. But in the international or global realm such an attitude is out of the question. Global aviation is not merely global in geographic concept. It will have to be global in its controls and in its entire organization and, in my opinion, it will have to operate under co-operative global direction.

The reader may well ask why such views should be held in relation to flight when every other means of communication has been developed by the private operator. The answer is simple. A period of ten days still elapses between the time of departure of a tramp steamer from the Hudson River and its arrival in the Mersey. Weeks elapse while a ship steams from San Francisco to the Antipodes. So it is with every form of surface transportation. Not so in the skies. Even today's multi-engined aircraft reach India from North America in a matter of thirty-six hours. Yesterday that journey involved weeks of tedious surface travel. The machines which make today's flights are obsolete *now* and they would be out of business tomorrow but for the fact that in war you cannot abandon production of what is available for immediate use and take time out to rebuild, retool, and reconstruct your whole aviation. But if the war should continue for another five years, do not imagine for a moment that it will be fought in the air by today's models of the Flying Fortress, the Liberator, the Lancaster, or the Wellington. So you may be sure that although aircraft in use at present may be called upon to bridge the gap of the immediate postwar period, if war should soon end, they will not be with us for long behind their present forms of propulsion. We are standing *now* in the doorway of stratospheric flight. We are on the threshold of the day when New York and Paris will be no more than three or four hours apart; in other words, the Atlantic is again about to shrink 75 per cent. In the not far distant future the businessman in a hurry will take his breakfast at home in the American Middle West, participate in a luncheon conference in London, and be back in his home in North America in plenty of time for dinner. How, then, can men of sense waste their own time and that of the people who listen to their opinions in contemplating aviation as they knew it in 1939, or even as we know it in 1944?

The question of controls of aviation in the world of tomorrow does not begin and end with matters of peaceable transportation. The threat lies in the military field. Are we going to permit nations so to develop aviation in a national sense that we shall live in a world armed to the teeth with lethal weapons, the like of which mankind has never known, or are we going to be sensible people and control our own and each other's activities in the skies? No question half so urgent will face the men who write tomorrow's treaties of peace.

My opinions concerning our German enemies of World Wars I and II have been set down fairly pungently in earlier chapters. Regardless of how much, or how little, the reader shares that opinion with me, the whole history of German aviation clearly proves that we cannot afford to underrate our enemies again. Some people are of the opinion that the only way in which we can find security in the air is by the strict maintenance of the policy of nationalism, as it is reflected in the idea of "closed sky." Others hold to the view that the solution lies at the other extremity, that is in complete freedom of the air, or "wide-open sky." Neither of these estimates is acceptable as it applies to our enemies, no matter the outcome between friends. In the first place, we are not going to be able to keep the German people on the ground for long, for the excellent reason that they will find a way to get back into the air. Perhaps we can find a way to grant them rights in a properly policed air (policed, that is, in the military sense); perhaps not. But one thing is sure: We cannot grant them freedom to operate with the connivance and assistance of people in our own countries as they did before, to sneak back into the sky while peace-loving men of good will are looking in the other direction, or are so engrossed in their private affairs as to lose interest in questions of safety. There can be no dummy companies in world aviation, and no behind-the-mulberry-bush manufacturing deals. To be safe we shall always have to know who's who in the air. Never again can we sacrifice safety to private profit.

Such statements apply with extreme force to our whole relationship with those who, as I write, are our enemies and to all our international relationships in the world of tomorrow. For our own safety, as a definite insurance policy against new wars, mankind can no longer tolerate under-cover arrangements as between cartels and other official and unofficial partnerships engaged in the manufacture of potentially lethal materials. There will always be men who, either from ignorance or selfishness, or a combination of the two, will be prepared to perform what may be termed acts of hostile manufacturing, solely for the purpose of private gain. That is one great reason why wars happen and it will apply in tomorrow's world with even greater force than in yesterday's if only because the world's productive capacity has increased so tremendously. The grim record of the basic matériel of war we passed on to our enemies, even during the days when we were virtually sure we would have to fight them again, and of the use of those supplies to kill our own sons is a matter of common knowledge today. It must never happen again. The view pronounced applies across the whole panorama of world relationships, but it applies with supreme force to our relationship with the people with whom we have been locked in a death-grip twice in a quarter of a century. We have got to learn this lesson sometime. It is only one lesson of many. But until we learn it no hope of an enduring peace may be found.

If we are going to live civilized lives tomorrow we must make sure that never again can the Germans be allowed to arm against us. This will include making sure that none of the greedy men in our own midst are given an opportunity to assist in the arming process, as they did between World Wars I and II.

But what are we going to do about each other? Are the present members of the United Nations themselves going to plunge headlong into an armaments race in which each will try to outdo the other with the air as the primary field of their war-like aspirations? Is any one of us going to outstrip all the others in the field of aerial development in the military sense? Is any one of us who is determined to be peaceable, or who acquires a government of appeasers, or who becomes convinced that he is safe behind an ocean barrier which has disappeared, going to lag behind the rest and suddenly wake up to discover that he is about to be annihilated from the skies? These are the things to which men must bend their most urgent thought as they dream of peace. These are the things that *can* happen here if we revert to the way of thinking which gave birth to the Treaty of Versailles, or if we attempt to write a new peace along nationalistic lines. No enduring peace lies that way. That way lies only the destruction of civilization. The world itself today is no greater than the continental United States of yesterday. Would the Governors of California and New York consider pitting their two states against each other on a battlefield somewhere in the Middle West? Of course they would not. Primarily they would not do so because the people of California and the people of New York know that they enjoy almost complete mutuality of interests; that, basically, what is good for one is good for the other; that prosperity for the people of California is likely to run parallel to prosperity for the people of New York; that both, in short, share a common goal. That mutuality of interest within the borders of the United States itself, or in Canada, or in any other land, is identical with today's and tomorrow's complete mutuality of world interest. In the Air Age what benefits Russia benefits America; what is good for Europe is good for Australia. What is required, then, is total acceptance of this axiom, coupled to the realization that we *dare* not again take up arms against each other.

What is to be said against something closely resembling world government and through it, world controls of world relationships? Not a thing can be said against such an approach to the future except that it is in conflict with man's own narrow views. We have all been brought up along narrow lines of nationalism and racism. As children we have been taught in the schools, and at the present time are teaching our own children, narrow and bigoted ideas about the rest of mankind. It is no easy matter to convince a man who, as a boy, learned about the American Revolution through nationalistic school textbooks, that he and his opposite number in Britain enjoy identical interests in the world of tomorrow. In Canada you can still find plenty of people who rejoice over the outcome of the pettifogging battles of the war of 1812, in which Canadian soldiers, dead these hundred years or more, were said to be victorious over aggressors from the United States. Strange to say, on looking between the covers of other books about the same war, published for the edification of American schoolboys, I discover that a totally opposite point of view is advanced and am told, in fact, that the Yanks licked us hollow. I offer this as a sample of the species of antiquated drivel which men to this day insist on instilling into their children. Relate the same kind of thinking to World War II and it takes the form of strange hosannas having to do with the "way of life" of this nation or that. Mr. Churchill's golden words have been adjudged by many of his auditors as meaning that the most important problem which faces people living in the British Nations is to save that Commonwealth and its interests, as such.

The strange debate concerning Russia's politico-economic system occupies the attention of other groups, some of which spend their time in apologizing for the way of life of our allies, others in trying to prove that the Soviet Union is democratic, others again in consigning Holy Russia and all its people to the nethermost depths of Gehenna. Yet such goings-on are relatively unimportant compared to the major question which we must resolve as we approach life in the Air Age.

It is important to me that the British Commonwealth of Nations shall continue to be what it is, perhaps with certain modifications, because I like the idea which is the motive power of the British partnership. It is only natural that an American boy fighting in the jungles of New Guinea should dream of his home in Iowa and be deeply convinced that it is the grandest place in the world and that nobody could dream up a better way of life than that which he hopes awaits him on his return to Main Street. It is equally natural that an officer in the Red Army should look forward to the day when he and his millions of brothers in arms will be able to return to the job of making a greater Russia.

But transcending all these logical, justifiable, and sensible aims and notions, one greater than all the rest is the concept of world citizenship, world co-operation, and world brotherhood for tomorrow. Without it we perish. No longer do men live at great distances from each other. We are sitting on each other's laps. I can afford to dislike a man who lives so far away from me that we cannot come to grips with each other without traveling for days or weeks to get into range. But I cannot afford to be on anything worse than speaking terms with my next-door neighbor, because he is in front of my eyes every day of my life and if I am going to spend my time quarreling with him, no time will remain to attend to all the things I want to do while I am here. That is the down-to-earth fact which faces the world. It is nearly as simple as that.

The scoffer inquires at this point: What do you mean when you say that Russia and America are next-door neighbors, when everybody knows they are separated by half the width of the world? The answers to such questions are not difficult to read—the answers are in the air. When men talk about stratospheric flight and the ability to fly from North America to Europe during the course of the morning they are not talking poppycock. They are talking about factors in the life of humanity with which we must come to grips at the very moment when we stop shooting at each other, or before the shooting stops if the war goes on much longer. Ponder, then, the new forms of propulsion which even now are in the air and flying. Then think of what their effect will be upon man's life in the future immediately ahead.

CHAPTER 2

Rush of Rocket and Thrust of Jet

FORTY years have elapsed since flight came to mankind from the natal manger of Kitty Hawk, forty years since man staggered into the air in box-kite contraptions which defied the law of gravity and set Fundamentalist true-believers to hoping that man's "challenge" to his Maker would be suitably answered by an angry Omnipotent Being. Since then we have gone on to fight two major wars in the skies, have developed the airplane as the supreme weapon of combat and destruction, and have paralleled this development with peaceable travel to anywhere. What lies ahead in aviation's next forty years, in its next twenty, in the decade immediately before us? Does aviation become the straight-line route to world peace through the skies; or does it go on from here to become a constant threat to our civilization through its use in the hands of aggressors? The choice lies with you and me, the ordinary everyday citizens of the world. What kind of weapon is it, then, that we have forged? Of what extent of destruction will it be capable tomorrow?

The airplanes in use today at the fighting fronts are capable of developing, as to fighters, speeds well in excess of 400 miles an hour. They pack multi-machine-gun punches in their wings and fire cannon through the hubs of their propellers. Those which flew in World War I, at first, carried no arms and traveled at 60 miles an hour. Those which flew on the day before the Armistice were capable of going no more than 140 miles an hour and they carried, at the outside, a couple of Vickers guns firing slowly in synchronization with the propeller blade. The bombers of World War I were gangling, rickety affairs, some still not unlike huge box kites, slow and carrying only light loads of projectiles to the target. In World War II Fortresses and Lancasters traveled to Fortress Europe, or to Jap-held Pacific islands, and lambasted the enemy with huge blockbusters aimed with considerable precision. Yet they are as obsolete (in that science is already running far before them) as your prewar automobile.

Let us take a quick recapitulating glance at the figures, choosing four important mileposts in the history of aviation—the beginning of World War I (1914), the end of World War I (1918), the beginning of World War II (1939) and the day when the freedom-loving nations invaded *Festung Europa* (June 6, 1944). From these we can catch a quick overall view of the tremendous surges which have taken place, each under the impact of war.[1]

---

[1] This chapter was written in the early spring of 1944. The tabulation comparing 1914, 1918, and 1944 air equipment was revised on June 14 in the futile hope of bringing the 1944 column up to date. On that day the United States Liberator (B-24) was considered a long-range, and the Flying Fortress (B-17) a medium-to-long-range, bomber. On June 15, the United States Government announced that Superfortresses (B-29's) had bombed Japanese islands, and released to the public a partial description of the world's mightiest bomber. Now the great Liberator (B-24) stepped down from its place of eminence and became a medium-range bomber, while the old Flying Fortress (B-17) was reclassified for use at short range. What had happened was not that the Liberator or the Fort had become less capable, but that the distances which men can fly non-stop in order to drop death-dealing missiles upon other human beings, and the power with which they can strike, had been, by the B-29, once more fantastically increased. The term "long range" had been given a new meaning.

Partial details of specifications and ability of the B-29 which the U. S. Government released on June 15 include:

Size: 98 feet long, 27 feet high, with a wingspan 141.2 feet, and four 16.5 foot propellers—half again as large as the B-17 Fortress or the Liberator.

Power: Four Wright Cyclone engines, each developing 2200 horse power—nearly twice that of the B-17.

Bomb capacity: Not revealed, save that the B-29 "carries a greater bomb load farther, faster, and higher, than any other airplane in existence."

Speed: Not announced, save as "300 miles an hour, plus."

Ceiling: Not announced, save that it is "well over 30,000 feet."

Armament: Not specifically announced, save as "multiple gun turrets, 50-caliber machine guns and 20-millimeter cannon."

Weight and range: "Very heavy and very long."

Fuel Capacity: More than that of a railroad tank car.

Operation: Entirely electrical, with the exception of hydraulic boosters on brakes, using 150 motors of 49 types. Electric power furnished by auxiliary engines. Special flight engineer—not pilot—controls power plant.

So important an advance is represented by the B-29 that a new fighting organization, the 20th Air Force, was created to utilize it "as the application of a new refinement of global warfare," according to the announcement of the U. S. War Department. So much for the knowledge of June 15, which made that of June 14 obsolete.

On June 16, the headlines of English language newspapers screamed: "Pilotless Nazi Plane Bomb! England Blasted by Hitler's Secret Weapon!" At this writing accurate knowledge of details of the new weapon are not available,

	1914	*1918*	*1939*	*1944*
Flying speed (in miles per hour)	60	130	320	450
Service ceiling (in feet).	8000	25,000	30,000	45,000
Engines (in horse power)	130	300	1000	2000 plus
Specific Weight per h.p. (in pounds)	4	2½	1½	1
Bomb-load carried (in pounds)	50	1800	4500	13,000
Offensive gun armament (in number of guns)	1	2	8	15 *
Defensive gun armament (in number of guns)	1	2	4	16 *

* All calibers are .303, excepting the 1944 column. Offensively in 1944 aircraft mounted one 75-mm. cannon plus fourteen .5 machine guns. Defensively they mounted sixteen .303 or eight .5 machine guns. In the larger bombers these were fired from four turrets in nose, tail, upper and lower fuselage.

Such a tabulation, of course, does not reveal the whole story and must be regarded solely as a hurried panoramic assessment. Today's guns, for example, are not merely of higher calibers than those of 1918, but each unit possesses double the striking power of its World War I predecessor, an average, say, of 500 rounds per minute in 1918 as compared to 1100 rounds in 1944. Nor is it possible to tabulate such items as radio and voice contact, virtually unknown in World War I, which enable aircraft to fight as closely knit teams, often under ground directions, today. New fuels, improved cooling systems, the addition of tremendous new aids to flight and navigation: all these and many other developments have lifted the fighting airplane of 1944 to a point at which its predecessors can barely find a basis of comparison. But . . .

Suppose we were to add another column to the table, heading it, say, 1954: what entries in terms of speeds, ceilings, horse power, and bomb-loads might it not reveal? If we visualize the whole presentation as a chart, the curve of which begins with the figures for

---

but first (and not necessarily accurate) accounts from Britain indicate that the weirdly terrifying infernal machine which swarmed across the Channel bringing death and destruction upon Southern England was a small, pilotless, possibly radio-controlled, jet- or rocket-propelled airplane carrying a bomb which exploded when the plane crashed against its target.

Can anyone who read the newspapers or listened to the radio during those two days in the history of aviation doubt the continuous and progressive obsolescence of all present aviation equipment, or fail to see the terrifying potentialities of man's conquest of the air?

1914 and climbs to those of 1918, then rises again to the record for 1939 and soars to 1944, the dotted line would then skyrocket up into the stratosphere, recording speeds at least equal to that of sound, with the aircraft itself, directed without human presence, functioning as the projectile (bomb-load). Such are the dizzying potentialities of the next decade.

But if, as I have said, our present planes are obsolete, why are the hard-hitting new weapons of air-power not in service today? The answer is simple. When the designer and the scientist who evolve an aircraft's motive power have worked through the labyrinths of invention to their target, that is merely a beginning, the longest stride to the destination, perhaps, but still only one step of many. A period of experimentation and testing must follow. Then comes another period of amendment and amelioration. Finally the most nearly perfect machine their labor can bring forth emerges. Only then can government and manufacturer begin to think in terms of tooling and only after a long period of tooling, bottleneck-busting, and preparation can they approach the final task of mass production. In all, a period of several years is likely to elapse between design and delivery to general uses. That is why the obsolescence of today's aviation is not immediately obvious. But it is certain that the new aviation is on the way. We can see what it is going to be even though we haven't yet arrived at the mass production stage.

Primarily, talk about what the aviation of tomorrow will be like focuses on new propulsion forms, called the jet and the rocket respectively. What are they? What can they do that the present arrangement of reciprocating-engine-plus-propeller will not do?

First, the jet, if only because it is likely to appear first in active service and is already in flight in Britain, in America, and probably in Germany. Sweden and Switzerland are other nations reported to be going all-out on jet-propulsion experiments at this time.

The principle of jet propulsion is identical with that of the propeller, in that the purpose of each is to produce a thrust which will drive an airplane forward by sucking in air and expelling it. In the case of the jet, however, the air is sucked in through an orifice, to be heated and expanded and ejected at high velocity through a nozzle, aft.

Considered alone, the jet holds several advantages over the engine-driven propeller. It has only about 10 per cent as many moving parts as the ordinary airplane engine. Hence it will be cheaper, more easily produced, and more easily kept running. It requires no ignition system, and ignition systems in the conventional engine must be pressurized at high altitudes. It has no carburetor and so needs no elaborate fuel-mixture controls. It presents no major icing problems. It needs no automatic throttle control, and it does away with the propeller. It does not need to be warmed up . . . just start the engines and away you go. It has other minor advantages and one disadvantage at its present stage of development. Its present extravagant fuel consumption offsets in some degree the lighter engine weight. But there are ways around *that* problem.

The idea of jet propulsion is not new. Engineers have been tinkering with it for centuries. Sir Isaac Newton is said to have invented and driven a jet-propelled horseless-carriage (with steam) as long ago as 1680. Call what has happened a job of adaptation and refinement and you will be somewhere near the mark.

The experiments which culminated in the acceptance of the first jet-impelled air fighter by Great Britain and the United States began in 1933, six years before the outbreak of World War II, under Group Captain Frank Whittle of the Royal Air Force. Four years passed before Whittle emerged from his shop with a satisfactory engine and the Air Ministry contracted with Gloster Aircraft to build a plane for Whittle to put it in. The resulting combination made its first satisfactory flights in England in 1941, at which time it was made available to the Americans, General Electric being commissioned to produce engines to Whittle's specifications and Bell Aircraft to do the job of turning out one or two prototype planes. The machine has now been test-flown in the United States, but is still a long way from the mass production line—this almost twelve years after Whittle went to work. But at least aviation men know the score, know what jet-propelled planes will do, and that jet propulsion is part of the why-and-how of the aviation of tomorrow, whether for war or peace. Refinement after refinement has been made during the testing period, both in Britain and in America. As matters stand at the time of writing, the position of the jet-propelled airplane, then, is something like this:

(1) It came along just about the time the propeller-type airplane seemed to be reaching its speed maximum.

(2) The practical ceiling of the propeller-driven plane was also in sight . . . propellers need something to bite on, and there is

no biteable substance in the thin air up near the stratosphere.

(3) The jet plane, therefore, brings higher speeds and altitudes into sight *now*. It is actually performing in these terms, with the experimental stage still not behind us.

Now about the rocket:

Much of what has been written in the press about rocket propulsion must have been extremely misleading to the layman, in that it has usually been accompanied by a picture of a strange-looking airplane being shot into the air like a giant firework, leaving the reader with a sort of general sense of whoosh and nothing much else to go on. Other stories have talked of series of rocket explosions as the plane hurtles through the stratosphere, and these give the reader a sort of staccato bang-bang-bang impression, as of an airplane moving forward swiftly in a series of terrifying jerks as each new firecracker explodes. This is not the picture at all.

The airplane of tomorrow, in sight today just out there on the hangar-apron behind that new jet-propulsion bird, will be something else entirely.

It will leave the ground smoothly impelled by rocket motors, which will assist its jet engines to get it off with huge loads, hitherto beyond our thinking. Once off, power will switch from the rocket engine to the jet engines, for the excellent reason that an airplane will fly comfortably with at least 50 per cent more load than it can take off the ground. The jets will attend to the provision of motive power until very high altitudes (in today's conception of altitude) are reached. Ultimately, however, the new aircraft will come into stratospheric altitudes in which the jet, requiring oxygen, will tire and finally quit. Then the rockets come into play again.

The rocket requires little, if any, atmosphere. I have listened to scientific friends discussing what will happen then. To simplify their erudite talk, I will simply put it that the plane will then thrust forward smoothly through the stratosphere at something faster than the speed of sound, and probably somewhere between 1000 and 1500 miles an hour. That will go on until the destination is, say, about 500 miles and thirty minutes away. Then the nose will turn down the long hill, and near the airport the jets will come into action and before the passenger in his air-conditioned and sound-proof cabin knows it, he will be back on *terra firma*, after crossing the Atlantic Ocean in three hours, perhaps less.

Fantastic, isn't it? But that is what is in sight. That is what the aero-scientists are up to in the here and now, not just dreaming about!

That is what is meant, then, by the repeated statement that the aircraft in use now are all obsolete, and by the other oft-repeated statement that mankind had better hurry and lift his social and political thinking into the realm in which he is going to be living, or else.

The conservative-minded, shut-in, afraid-of-change person may take fright as he looks at the awesome picture of tomorrow's rocket-and-jet superstratospheric airplane. No need to do so. What we have to be afraid of, rather, is our own lack of capacity for proper use of such instruments. There is nothing wrong with the instruments, as such, but only with man's outlook.

If the problem of the air in the world of tomorrow were to be bounded solely by aviation as we knew it in 1939, or by the geography of the prewar flat-map world, perhaps mankind would not have too much to worry about as he looks ahead and plans for peace. Even under these conditions our problems would be manifold, for it is primarily during the years of the present war that we have finally conquered the oceans and become able to move from continent to continent by air year-in and year-out, virtually every day of the year. But if we look at the revolution of the air which took place between 1914 and 1939, realizing that we came in that brief period from the day of the box kite to the day of the multi-engined transocean airliner, and then look at what has happened during the course of World War II, the reader will soon realize that we must cope with forces in the world of tomorrow which call for an entirely new approach, that of world-thought and a completely new set of human values. Mankind was never extremely successful in the realm of preserving the peace before the dawn of the Air Age. Can we expect any improvement under the conditions we shall face tomorrow?

Jet propulsion, coupled finally to the rocket, will open the realm of the upper stratosphere to the flying machine. In days to come planes will travel at enormous heights, at something approximating the speed of sound, or faster, consuming infinitesimal amounts of fuel, carrying loads hitherto undreamed of, and, if necessary, directed from points of take-off to points of landing by radio and electronic devices. Compare this with the performance of today's four-engined bomber, with such aircraft as the American DC4 or Britain's Lancaster, and you immediately face the fact that the revolution destined to take place between today and tomorrow is even greater than that which happened between 1914 and 1939, or, if you prefer, between yesterday and today. The scientist has thrown open yet another in the series of doorways into the higher heavens and the implications of what that open doorway means to mankind almost beggar the imagination, primarily because virtually all men still think in groundbound terms.

When you stop to remember that Britain had no accurate radio-location device in the autumn of 1939, whereas today she can pick up with complete accuracy through the medium of such devices enemy aircraft which are still far from her coasts and pin-point them all the way in for the anti-aircraft gunners and air fighters, you are thinking of just one of many immeasurable advances which have taken place in these brief years of war. Or, consider the gifts of science which enable the gunner on the ground to get on his target in the skies with unerring accuracy. Knowing these things, all fragmentary pieces of the Revolution of the Air Age, can you logically refuse to believe that anything can happen tomorrow—and probably will?

Can you visualize tremendous armadas of aircraft which themselves may be projectiles, launched from the ground by rocket impulsion, then carried to their destination by means of jet propulsion and more rocket-impulses, their whole course of flight directed by the press of a button on the ground?[1] Can you imagine such air projectiles launched from a point in Europe and arriving in America three hours later? Can you imagine the threat to the civilization in which we live today which is contained in the possibility of the ultimate forms of development of such weapons?[1]

Now think about war. Every American and every European knows only too well by this time that the day of formally declared war is a thing of the past. Our enemies have not even been too fussy about their manners in this respect in the immediate past. Long before her attack on Pearl Harbor, Japan marched in on

[1] This was written two months before Germany launched what apparently is exactly this kind of device against England, on June 16, 1944. I have not revised the question, both because accurate knowledge of the details of the German plane-projectile is not available as this book goes to press, and because the speculation and the confirming fact form such an excellent example of the fantastic speed which continues to mark the advance of aviation.

Manchuria and on the Chinese under flimsy pretexts of defending the hapless residents of those areas from somebody else's mythical aggression. When Hitler overran Poland he began by the simple expedient of turning the *Luftwaffe* and the panzers loose across its borders. So too when he attacked Russia. No aggressor nation, once it has become sufficiently powerful to satisfy the appetites of aggression, ever again will bother about the niceties of declaring war. In future such an aggressor will simply unleash the full power of his stratospheric air projectiles. The first warning his simple-minded enemies will receive of his intention to attack will be when a defender's detection devices tell him that those projectiles are on their way across the intervening space—whether land or sea—and they will be exploding in the heart of his capital in a matter of hours at the outside, perhaps in minutes. With luck the peace-lover may just have time to duck for cover a thousand feet underground. Huge cities could be reduced to rubble and ashes in a single sortie. You might almost say that, if we are going to have any more wars, we had better be about the business of turning New York's skyscrapers up-side-down *now* and burrowing deep down into the ground to live like moles in the hope of finding precarious security. As the science of the air tends to develop, its powers of destruction and devastation will become so great as to convert areas of almost any size into ruins with a single massed blow from the air.

It may be argued that our scientists will provide other instruments of death to counterbalance such fantastic weapons. Perhaps so. The question would then seem to arise: Is this to be the final pass to which civilized man reduces his civilization? Is it our purpose to bring on war after war after war, until the horror of the cataclysm becomes so great that everything we have ever built of good is to be destroyed and ourselves with it? It will do us no good to call these things fantastic, or for our leaders to play ostrich again. Mankind is on the spot. Only the most careful application of intelligence and energy can get us off it.

Speaking of matters fantastic, you may recall a man named Jules Verne who wrote a book many years ago telling us all about the submarine. It was a book of sheer fantasy and the so-called "conservative man of good sense" (which is just another name for people who live in terror of change and never dare look it in the eye, even when it happens) branded it as being so far outside the realm of the comprehension of any sane person as to be beyond consideration. Since then we have had two world wars, in each of which we have been hard put to it to deliver war supplies to the battlefields or to feed civilian populations in an embattled Europe, simply because the Germans were able to send a couple of hundred of these deadly underwater engines of war to sea to attack and sink our ships. Fantastic, wasn't it?

Shortly before World War I, an English author of thrillers, who wrote under the name of William LeQueux, turned out a book called *When It Was Dark*. In it LeQueux pictured an entirely mythical Zeppelin raid on New York City, and depicted the horrors and complete dislocation of human life which the great gasbags, turned loose without warning, could bring to bear on a crowded city. True, the Zeps did not come to New York during World War I, nor have they, or any other airborne machines (up to the time of this writing), bombed the North American continent during the course of World War II. But almost before the ink was dry on the pages of LeQueux's book, these same huge airships were raining down bombs on the civilian population of London and other English cities, and for many months the Royal Flying Corps was hard put to it to solve the riddle of how to cope with them. Fantastic, wasn't it?

In the Age of Science, in the Air Age, today's fantasy is tomorrow's reality. That has been proved so many times, with such extremely painful results to the unbeliever, that the time has passed to refrain from discussing what may appear to thc uninitiated as fantastic, for fear of being adjudged a lunatic. Far better to discuss it and examine what *can* happen. That way you get no sand in your eyes from burying your head in a dune.

The primary object of such talk is to bring home the thought that we can no longer afford the bitter luxury of war. Civilian populations, women and children by the thousands, tens of thousands of old men and women in their declining years, were destroyed during the course of the Second World War by weapons their leaders pretended did not exist, or with which we pretended we could cope without trouble. Have the men who permitted Germany and Japan to arm, who helped them to do so, or who failed at least to arm us, ever accepted their responsibility? Indeed they have not. All they have ever done is to say that we, the People, are to blame for not having forced them to act. But do we allow the defaulting teller to plead that the president of the bank is to blame for the clerk's embezzlements, because he let him have money in the till to dish out to the bank's customers? Indeed, no. We punish the teller as a betrayer of the trust the bank, its shareholders, and depositors placed in him.

In future wars civilian populations will be at the mercy of any aggressor, for aggression will come without warning and its impact will be so terrific that what has happened to Europe during World War II will be picayune by comparison. One shudders, therefore, as one contemplates the backward thinking of so many of the world's leaders, so much of its influential press and, as a result, of so many of the ordinary men and women of good will with whom the world abounds. Are we going to permit the new weapons of the air to run wild in our world, or are we going to bring them under man's control? If the former, the world is not going to be a comfortable place in which to be about twenty-five years hence. If the latter, it is completely within our power, but only if enough of us think and act in world terms, and scuttle all the leaky craft of narrow nationalism. If we have the broadness of vision and the courage to parallel the Revolution of the Air Age with the Revolution of Mankind, we shall establish a finer civilization than we have ever known, a civilization in which man's primary servant and ally will be aviation, whereas otherwise it will be his enemy and the tool of the aggressor.

CHAPTER 3

Winged Peace or Winged Death

AS THE United Nations come down the home stretch toward victory, men begin to look ahead in hope to an end to carnage and the writing of an enduring peace. Men tell each other that the future of all mankind rests on four cornerstones, the United States, the British Commonwealth, the Soviet Union, and China, and that the great nations must accept the responsibilities of their greatness and in turn share with the smaller nations and the liberated peoples a common brotherhood. These are the idealistic things of which we speak and of which our press continually writes. But are these the terms in which we are actually thinking?

As you look about you and listen to some of the greatest leaders in the United Nations, there begins to be discernible and audible a definite swing back to the nationalism which pervaded the atmosphere of the 1930's. With victory in sight and, we say, assured, our approach to partnership is by no means as selfless and generous as when we walked together in dire adversity.

When France fell and the British nations stood alone, it is much more than possible that the Commonwealth, of which my country is a member, was saved and human liberty itself granted a new lease on life through the generosity of the people of the United States, who gave unsparingly of the product of factory and field to make sure that the island bastion of Britain should not fall. Men of ungenerous mind might say that Uncle Sam himself had one eye on the weather. It could be argued that the material and food sent forward from the United States was sent because far-sighted men, like President Roosevelt and many others, believed that the salvation of the United States itself hinged in large degree on keeping Britain fighting. Otherwise the final phases of the battle might be for and in the Americas. That is all quite true. But it was not the vital reason which brought American aid to the British people. What drove America forward, step by step, from cash-on-the-barrelhead to Lend-Lease, to the American Navy's watch-and-ward over the Atlantic, to the establishment of convoys and finally to "all aid short of war," was the deep feeling of kinship between the common man in the United States and the common people of Britain; the admiration of the American people, as people, for the courage of the British people in their determination to die rather than come to terms with Hitler. If that feeling had not existed, not even a Roosevelt could have sent help. Our partnership, in short, springs from brotherhood, a brotherhood we must keep in the days to come.

So too with our attitude to Russia, after Germany invaded the Soviet Union in the summer of 1941. In this case there was much greater opportunity for misunderstanding and hanging back than in the case of the United States and Britain. We had come through a period of misunderstanding dating back to the days of the Russian Revolution, which we had ourselves attempted to quell by force of arms. For almost twenty-five years we had entertained toward the Soviet Union ideas in large degree fashioned on misrepresentation. Underlying the realities, the whole relationship was confused by the clash of political and economic systems. Before 1939 Russia had decided to go her own way without us, because we refused her co-operation and even barred her from attending the so-called "conference" at Munich. We had consigned Russia *and her people* to the uttermost depths of hell for the pact made with Hitler shortly before the outbreak of World War II. Yet when the Germans stepped across the borders of the Soviet Union we rushed to her aid as best we could. Despite the tangled jungle of bigotry and misunderstanding through which we marched to help, a deep admiration of the spirit of the fighting Russian people welled up in us, an admiration which thrust aside every last vestige of the hostility we had nurtured for years.

Then came another example of the warm brotherhood which has motivated all of us as partners in war. Canada had drawn strength from its great neighbor while the Dominion was at war and the Republic was not actually so. We had entered into a hard-binding pact of mutual defense. We had interlocked our economies. Although Canada was not a participant in Lend-Lease, because the staunchly independent Canadian people believed that they could pay their own way, finance their own war effort, and aid their allies through the medium of closely controlled internal economy, we had nevertheless drawn largely on the resources of the United States. The fact that Canada was able to pay her bills in no way detracted from the generosity of American help. But the greatest assistance which came Canada's way from her neighbor had been that of the American people themselves. Young Americans had hastened across the border in thousands to enlist and fight under the banner of Canada. That was the greatest contribution of all, for it was a contribution born of our brotherhood and kinship, and it is one no Canadian will ever forget.

Canada's opportunity to repay in the coin of brotherhood came on the day the Japanese bombed Pearl Harbor. Not much has ever been said about what happened and much of what happened must remain secret until the war is behind us. But it can be said that in that hour the United States found itself in some respects as badly off as Britain had been the day after the last ferry-boat and unarmed yacht left the beaches of Dunkirk. Immediately the United States forces found themselves woefully short of ammunition. Canada put its supplies at Uncle Sam's disposal and in a matter of hours freight cars in hundreds on the Canadian side of the border were being loaded with shells, small arms ammunition, and all manner of gun-food while the Dominion's explosives plants were turned into double high gear to produce more and more munitions for its neighbors and allies. Guns went from the Dominion to forces in the Pacific theater. Within two or three days fleets of bombers were leaving Canadian soil loaded with materials which the United States lacked in sufficient quantity for its defense. Canada dipped into its man-power resources and returned to their native land 2000 flying men then wearing the uniform of the R.C.A.F. Perhaps Canada did not send as much as some Canadians would like it to be thought was sent. But the point is that whatever Canada had on hand that the United States needed was immediately put at the neighbor's disposal. Not one word of this is said in any braggadocial sense. It is said humbly, simply as testimony to the sense of neighborship and brotherhood extended mutually across the imaginary line in hours of extremity.

The whole relationship of the United Nations had found its sustenance in mutual generosity. Long before the United States was at war the military secrets and formulas of Englishmen, Australians, and Canadians were made available to their opposite numbers in Washington. An example in point is that of the powerful explosive known as RDX, which had been made usable in Britain but was developed by Canadian scientists for more effective use. Long before Pearl Harbor, Canadians carried their RDX to Washington, where absolutely nothing was known of the substance. Thenceforward Canadian and American chemists, working hand in hand, developed and were responsible for the ultimate formula which has given RDX 40 per cent more wallop than any other explosive in use by the United Nations.

In other words, we have all worked hand in hand, each giving freely to the others, having no secrets from one another, working together for one common purpose—total victory. Nowhere in man's history may such evidence be found to support the view that men can work together in harmony for the common good of all. Up to now, however, our instincts of brotherhood flower only in adversity. Can we carry this glorious partnership of the United Nations forward into a world of peace? Can we maintain in peace the partnership we have fashioned and shared in war?

As we approach victory, grit begins to scratch the gears of partnership. Now that we begin to feel secure in our belief in victory, now that we know in our hearts that we cannot lose, men begin to turn again to the irritants of nationalism, to the petty bigotries and the destroying selfishnesses which are the causes of all wars. As this is written, this outlook is reflected mainly in minor things, perhaps, but it cannot be denied that a great many people are resurrecting the petty hostilities of yesterday. Nations are beginning to talk in terms of the selfish interests they threw aside like old shoes when they were in danger. Every force responsible for the manufacture of wars is coming to life again. It cannot go on or we shall lose another peace and, sooner or later, fight again.

These irritants are definitely felt in the realm of world aviation, a realm in which we must all move with the greatest care and with the greatest respect for each other's needs and security. Perhaps we can afford to squabble about minor matters, but we certainly cannot afford to live in anything but the closest accord once we leave the ground in international flight.

What are the points of disagreement about the air? Basically there are none which matter a snap of the fingers, but, unfortunately, governments are being egged on by selfish interests inside their own countries. The approach is rapidly degenerating into a determination on every nation's part to "get what is coming to it," more if it can do so. As this is written we are heading straight back toward the same old sovereignty ideas which governed the air before we began to use it together in self-defense. We are perhaps not taking exactly the same direction. Even the most violent air-grabbers among us would refute the suggestion that aircraft of one country should be able to land on the soil of another country only on the stringent terms we used to know. "Enlightened self-interest" is taking a new tack today, but its destination has not changed. We might as well be extremely frank about it, because the issues at stake are of too great importance for any of us to attempt to evade them. What is going on is every bit as nationalistic in its approach as the old sovereignty policy. There are air operators and politicos in the United States who are determined that American aviation shall dominate that of the world. A similar pronouncement is applicable to similar interests in Britain—and such interests are extremely powerful in both countries. In due course, no doubt, Russia will be putting forward her own ideas. One by one aircraft interests in what are now the occupied and neutral countries will soon follow our example. Finally demands will even be received from our enemies for a share of the spoils. The whole thesis of this approach is utterly wrong. Global aviation not only will *not* work under such conditions; the only outcome of such methods will be to lead us back to international ill will and, finally, to grave international disputes and trouble. No man of good will can support a world-aviation operated by profit-seeking individuals and founded on the dog-eat-dog theory of commerce. The air (other than in the domestic sense) is *not* national. The air is global and the operator of tomorrow in the global air must be a global operator. No words can be minced about it. The air-world must be world-controlled.

Much talk goes on about the controls of the air which are to be exerted in a world of peace and by whom those controls are to be exerted. Mostly the talk has not been projected beyond the realm of nationalistic thinking. Shortly before these paragraphs were written, Britain aligned itself, through the spokesmanship of Lord Beaverbrook, with the school of thought in the United States which talks in terms of free-for-all competition, as opposed to the views advanced by Canada for an international control body which would enjoy broad powers in allotting airlines and in the enforcement of a world air agreement, or series of agreements. More hopeful, from the point of view of those who know the inflammable nature of the air problem, has been the attitude of the Labour Party in Britain, which speaks in terms of what may be described as a world air transport company in which the nations would be partners. It is my own profound conviction that the task of organizing our use of the air after the war is essentially that of such an organization. I do not see how we can do otherwise, without risking new misunderstandings ultimately disastrous to the future peace of man, misunderstandings which will ultimately divide us on issues of narrow national interest.

It is not for me to attempt to tell either the United States or the United Kingdom how they should view the future of the Air Age. That would be presumptuous on my part and I have no doubt it would be so regarded. I have come to realize the power of the air, however, and, conversely, its tremendous potentialities of use for the good of all mankind. Hence, with the utmost vehemence at my command, I must plead the case for world cooperation and organization, before we blunder again into new cataclysms. We shall so blunder if we embark on any high, wide, and handsome scrambling for air routes in the world of tomorrow.

At the outset of this book the whole question of geography of the Air Age was examined and discussed. The attempt was made to prove that the whole geography of our world has been revolutionized by the airplane. Certainly the focal center of the world today lies in the two great northern land masses and certainly it is in those two areas that the great developments of tomorrow for good or ill will take place. As a person living in the northern half of North America, extremely close to the center of gravity of the Air Age, I naturally have the keenest interest, and something greater than interest, in the means we are to use in organizing and controlling the air. The whole approach to transportation and communication changes at the moment one begins to think in terms of Air Age geography.

Throughout the war, members of the United Nations living at points thousands of miles away from the battlefields have been forwarding daily great tonnages of war supplies—precious scientific equipment and instruments, secret strategic materials, and all manner of vitamins and medical supplies—from continent to continent by air. The scores of thousands of aircraft built in North America during the war, and rushed forward to the fighting fronts were all self-delivered excepting those of extremely short range. Huge bodies of men are moved to the battlefronts by glider. Loaded gliders have been towed non-stop from Canada to Britain. Mechanized vehicles for use on the ground often are carried by air to the scene of action. Yet all manner of wiseacres insist we shall never do any important peacetime shipping of goods by air and that people will always prefer to travel by ship when they set out to visit faraway countries. Don't be too sure. Remember the merchants of Genoa and Venice. I expect to live to see the day when the people of the nations will visit back and forth by air as freely as our parents used to visit neighbors in the next township. Aviation, therefore, will immediately become the greatest educator the world has ever known and our first sure highway to mutual understanding as between peoples.

Obviously, then, we need a new book of rules for a brand new style of communications. What should those rules be and who will make them? Will they be drawn up and enforced by the great powers alone or will the smaller nations have a say in the matter?

Take Canada, for instance, whose geographic position gives her a peculiar interest in the problem and a peculiar advantage in any future planning of the world's airways. The world cannot turn a deaf ear to Canada's views, for the excellent reason that nobody in the Northern Hemisphere, nobody living on the northern land mass, can do much about international aviation unless he has the freedom of use of the air over the North American Dominion. If people living elsewhere in the Americas, in Europe, or in Asia are desirous of establishing air ties, they must enjoy the freest possible air liaison with the Dominion of Canada. It is possible, of course, to fly from New York to London, or New York to Moscow, or from Chicago to the Orient, or in the other direction over any of these routes, and avoid Canadian air and soil, but it is not convenient, and, therefore, would be economically unsound. Canada stands at the center of the crossroads of the world's main air highways. Therefore it is only reasonable to assume that the peoples of Russia, Britain, the United States, and of virtually every other country lying north of the equator, must enjoy "air friendship" with the Canadian people and access to Canadian ground facilities (if only in cases of emergency), and to free use of the air over Canadian soil. Therefore it is of supreme importance that Canada should have stated its position in respect of global aviation as definitely being that of air co-operation, not simply an approach of what's-in-it-for-me?

But about the rules.

What I have to say does not pretend to reflect the opinion of the Canadian Government, or of any political party in the Dominion, or of anyone but myself as an individual who has spent all his adult life in aviation and whose friends in aviation live in almost every country under the sun.

What is needed in the air goes even beyond the realm of world rules and world controls. What is required is *world operation of world airways*. That is the only feasible program for global aviation.

Nobody knows what form of world society of nations we shall create at the peace table, whether we shall attempt to do a repaint and overhaul job on the old League of Nations, equipping it with the teeth it always needed so badly, or whether we shall attempt some entirely new form of world government. Such a world government could have been established with ease when the United Nations had their backs against the wall. Then the idea of world union was on every man's lips. But we have slipped badly since the circumstances of war took a turn for the better. I am one of those who stand convinced that we must create some form of supreme world organization if we are to have enduring peace. Assuming that we shall create such a body, that body must not merely *control* intercontinental and international flight—it should *direct* it and *operate* it.

The directors of such an organization would be representatives of the respective countries, and countries perhaps would be given representation based on populations, or shares of world trade, or geographical situation, or other factors. Nobody should be excluded. World-air personnel from the top down to the lowest grease-monkey should be men trained to think in world terms, men of world loyalties. All aircraft flying the global routes would fly under the ensign of the world-air organization. It must be alone and supreme in global aviation and the purpose of its operations should not be commercial or profit-making. If we *must* be obsessed by the idea of profit, then the profits of such an operating world company should go into the treasury of whatever the world league or world government of tomorrow is going to be. All this is no more than an attempt to put the outline of an idea down on paper. At this time it is fundamentally an idea. The terms and details can be worked out later. What is required *now* is that all nations, beginning with the Big Four, but taking in all of us, should move to accept the principle of such a formula. They should do so for the excellent reason that any other policy or program will quickly prove itself unworkable and is bound to lead to international dispute and ill will.

Why do I regard the air of the world as global property, and the use of that air as requiring an outlook of global partnership? I do so solely because I can think of no other way in which we can make use of the air globally without courting disaster.

Such matters, of course, raise the question of what controls are to be exerted over the air of the world in the military sense, if what we want is an enduring era of world peace. Early in this book I made the remark, and italicized it, that *we shall have to trust each other in the air.* We must construct an edifice on the cornerstone of world trust, and the nation or the man who betrays that trust must be jumped on like a ton-of-bricks by everybody else and punished for his breach of trust at the moment when he first betrays it. The League of Nations was going to do something like that. The trouble with the League, of course, was not its constitution but the kind of men who foregathered in Geneva to make its decisions, and the selfishness of the interests they served. The League had powerful weapons in its hands. Its members simply did not choose to use them. They refused to impose sanctions on Mussolini when he raped Ethiopia. They blinded their eyes to Japanese aggression in Manchuria. They refused to have anything to do with the Loyalist Government of Spain. They refused to stand four-square against aggressors when to do so could have nipped aggression in the bud. The League idea, as conceived, was valid and honorable. The League itself became impotent and without honor because its members refused to stand firm to maintain the peace of the world, but always gave support to selfish interests. But nothing was ever wrong with the concept of the League, except that its constitution was riddled with escape-hatches.

So the League, or something very much like the League, is our proper step. This time, however, we must make it, in every sense of the term, a true world government, governing for man. Whatever its other functions will be, it must control world aviation, both military and civil.

Let me now proceed to put my head squarely into the mouth of the nationalistic lion in every country in the world.

The question is already widely discussed as to what air strengths each nation should or will have and how these should be limited. The only solution is to get rid of them. If we have "limited" national air forces, somebody will always break the limit. As long as we have national air forces we shall have groups, blocs, cartels of nations, privately and secretly undertaking to hang together and in due course blow the top off other blocs or groups. This is the end result of power diplomacy and power politics and it has been going on since the beginning of time. So has war. Are men desirous of putting an end to carnage? Well, we cannot rid ourselves of war without first getting rid of international power groups in all their selfish ugliness and unless, as a starting point, we control all aviation by making it a world force. Aviation is too dangerous a weapon for stupid or selfish people to possess for their personal use.

World military aviation must be a world organization. The loyalties of its members must be world loyalties. It must be a strong force. To be a member of it, to wear its uniform, to hold its commission, must be the highest honor to which a young man may aspire. It will police the world. It would not waste one moment in talking before raising plain, ordinary hell with anybody in the world who committed any infraction of the rules of peace, in fact or in spirit.

So, too, with the industrial aspects of aviation as they affect its military side. So, too, with the developments of science in the realm of flight and the facilities which make flight possible and safe. The product of the air scientists' minds must be available to all men in all nations. No manufacturer of military aircraft can be allowed to manufacture military air equipment for anyone but the World Air Force.

What is being hammered home is that we have in our hands the most potent weapon ever invented by man. Consistently it becomes more potent. It will continue to become more potent as the years go by. Therefore we must have steel-trap controls which we can spring at a moment's notice on any potential aggressor or on selfish men, traitors to the thesis of world brotherhood and to mankind's desire for peace.

Into this whole panorama of the Air Age of tomorrow, fraught as it is with unassessable dangers, comes a realization of the boons to be conferred on mankind through the air, if mankind is ready to become *homo sapiens* and cease to be a dolt always ready to pick up a gun and start shooting.

We can use the air for peace even as widely as we can use it for destruction. Tomorrow I hope our young citizens, in hundreds and thousands, will fly from country to country and come to know each other, come to know the lore and traditions of each other's native lands, and, what is more important, enjoy the free exchange of ideas which is only possible when people can meet face to face, talk to each other and live together.

Somebody says: "Who is going to pay the freight? Who is going to buy the airplane tickets? Who is going to supply the expense money for all this getting around the world and getting to know each other?" Is this to be the crux of the question? It has been said repeatedly in these pages that world aviation cannot be restricted to the narrow confines of commerce-for-profit. There is no valid reason why a boy in England or a girl in the United States should be without opportunity to find out about each other's countries simply because the two young people happen to come from humble circumstances. Unfortunately, political and social thinking stand almost precisely where they stood when the first airplane flew at Kitty Hawk, whereas science has moved forward by leaps and bounds to create an abundance of facilities for man's use. Man must avail himself of them, for if we do not make constructive, peaceable use of them, in time we shall put them to destructive, war-like use.

The governments of the United States, of Canada, Russia, Britain, or any other country within the United Nations partnership, do not give a moment's thought to the expense involved in transporting thousands of people from one side of the world to the other for the purpose of destroying our enemies. We call this the necessity of war. Has peace no necessities? What is wrong then with the idea of moving people in equally great numbers over similar distances for the purpose of neighborly peace? I am one of those peculiar people who stand convinced that peaceable missions are worth more to us than war-like missions and that if we spend our resources to build up world peace and brotherhood we can avoid the horror and expense in lives and resources of future wars. Let it stand at that!

Most people still believe that we are fighting to retain, or to get back, what we had in 1938. In a great many of us the idea is deeply rooted that the great problem which faces all men is the strange politico-economic tussle between capitalism and socialism. I have already pointed out that this question is secondary to that of civilization's survival. But I do know that if one group of nations insists upon encouraging and supporting bigoted opinion about the way of living of another group, sooner or later somebody will shoot somebody else. Then the rockets will fly. And all hell will be let loose. If, on the other hand, the people of our shrunken world are given opportunity to know each other, it is my conviction that any dispute born of such addled thinking will collapse for want of support.

In other words, we can live on *our* side of the new Mediterranean and Russia on *its* side, each keeping its own political and economic outlook, as applicable to itself, each developing its own resources but making them available to the other, each without interfering with the manner in which the people on either side of the North Pole want to live, or to govern themselves.

We can retain our traditions, our customs, our ways of life, each in his own country, each amending his way of life, economically or politically, from time to time as circumstances demand, without engaging in external interferences or disputes leading to war. We can only do so, however, in an atmosphere of mutual trust and cooperation *outside the field of domestic affairs.* We can do so only if we recognize and accept the implications of world citizenship, superimposed on national citizenship, holding under closest control the means to destruction inherent in aviation and developing our aviation for the good of all men and the peace of the world.

The Air Age faces mankind with a sharp choice—the choice between Winged Peace or Winged Death.

It's up to you.

A F T E R W O R D

Left Unsaid

by Arthur Bishop

INSIDE the cover of the copy of *Winged Peace* from which this republished version of the book has been reprinted, a handwritten inscription in Russian for my wife Priscilla reads: "To the most beautiful girl in the world."

When on the evening of May 3, 1945 (her birthday), 'Cilla asked my father to autograph it, he was only too glad to oblige, provided it could be done with a difference, a flair. The ordinary never satisfied him. He always insisted on that extra mile. In this case he decided that nothing less than an inscription in the Soviet language would suffice.

In a sense it was logical, if you can call it that. At the time, we lived on the corner of Laurier and Blackburn avenues in Ottawa. Several houses away on the same street was a branch of the Russian Embassy. As his aide, *ex officio* (we were both still in uniform, pending discharge from the R.C.A.F.), I accompanied him down and across the street to the Embassy; we were greeted suspiciously at the door by a burly, great bear of a six-foot-five male receptionist. Brandishing the copy of *Winged Peace*, my father asked if there was someone at home who could write something in it in Russian.

Not understanding English and bewildered at the sight of two uniformed officers suddenly appearing on the doorstep, the receptionist seemed nonplussed. Impassive, but nonplussed. In the light of subsequent events, he was probably not only perplexed but downright scared. Nevertheless, he beckoned us inside and gestured us to be seated while he sat himself behind a desk and made a telephone call.

I was struck by the overpowering atmosphere of Spartan gloom in the oak-panelled hall, which was draped in heavy burgundy-coloured curtains. A huge framed picture of Stalin dominated the room. My father jerked a thumb toward the massive portrait and commented to the Russian, "Good old Uncle Joe." No reaction. None. None at all.

After several minutes the telephone rang. Big Bear answered it with something that sounded like a couple of *Da*'s; he then pressed a button on the side of the desk, whereupon all hell broke loose. A shuffle of feet and a babble of voices as at least twenty men and women came scurrying down the stairs that abutted the hall and disappeared through a doorway, presumably down to the basement. My father grinned. Mischievously he muttered, "I think we've broken up some sort of a party."

But Big Bear never even nodded a *nyet* through it all. And he was probably the one who had activated the affair. He seemed completely absorbed in some papers he had on his desk. I walked over and had a look. He was filling out an illustrated lesson in English. The paper showed a drawing of an object; on one side of it was a word in Russian, on the other, a blank space to fill in the corresponding English word. For something to do while we waited, I offered to help him by filling in the word and, for the first time since we arrived, he smiled.

About half an hour later, the front door opened and a well-dressed man walked in. He introduced himself with a name I could hardly understand—and quickly forgot—and in broken, but articulate, English asked what he could do for us. We made our request and he politely complied. And after writing the inscription in the book, he apologized for not having anything in the house to offer us to drink. He explained that he had just walked over from the Russian Embassy, which was three blocks away, hence the delay. We thanked him and left.

The exercise was completely forgotten until the Gouzenko defection burst upon the world the following year. It then became shudderingly clear that we had almost walked into part of the Soviet atomic espionage operation. I have long since wondered what part poor old Big Bear had in it. And if he had had a part in it, could I be charged with complicity for helping him with his English?

In any case, that experience became known *en famille* as the "Winged Peace Incident." It went beyond the mere delineation of a joke, however. In light of the Russian threat, it crystallized in the minds of all of us in the family what the book had meant to attain because it cast it into fresh perspective. Now the world stood at the check-in point of a new peril. *Winged Peace* had been originally intended as a legacy to those who had and would serve the interests of aviation both militarily and commercially. Perhaps now it had been given an added dimension. How well, then, has it served those aims, those purposes?

My father was very disappointed in the reaction to his work when it first hit the bookstores. He had expected, and wanted, to create a controversy. Practically speaking, that sells books. But, as an author and a visionary, he had hoped to overcome what he most feared aviation might invite after so many long years of war: complacency and greed—and, perhaps, as a result, another world conflict. In effect, he wanted to be challenged, to be taken to task for his deliberations. But that just didn't happen. His fame, reputation, and stature gave him too much eminence as an aviation authority to create the argument he had wished to incite. Certainly, enough material lay open to debate and question; and many conclusions were drawn with which to take issues. Yet nobody took up the cudgel. Reviews, both in the United States and Canada, were not only favourable, but many were highly laudatory.

So if in *Winged Peace* there are areas still open to discussion, how do the tenets that Billy Bishop advanced, towards the end of his tenure as a serving senior military air officer, measure up today nearly four decades after the initial publication of *Winged Peace*? Let's examine some of the more contentious passages.

> The solution of international air relationships must be completely divorced from the private profit instinct. If it is not so divorced and if we plunge into any form of traffic war as between nations, the only possible outcome is trouble for all concerned. . . . Each country will probably operate its own internal and local aviation through the medium of private commerce, or by any other means it chooses. But in the international or global realm such an attitude is out of the question. . . . It will have to be global in its controls, in its entire organization and, in my opinion, it will have to operate under co-operative global direction.

This precept became activated a lot quicker than the author could have hoped, and Canada played a key part. By 1946, under Sir William Hildred, I.A.T.A. (International Air Transport Association) had set up headquarters in Montreal. The Association became the pivotal point for governing standardization of the function of the airlines within the United Nations. At the outset, its task to establish uniformity was manifold: type of equipment, procedures, language, signals—even customs clearances. Indeed, over the years it established, not without a share of headaches, the global direction that Bishop Sr. deemed necessary: "What do you mean when you say that Russia and America are next-door neighbours, when everybody knows they are separated by half the width of the world? . . . The answers are in the air."

Communications with the U.S.S.R. available through the medium of air travel (i.e., personal face-to-face parley within hours), kept the Cold War, even at its peak, within negotiable parameters.

> When men talk about stratospheric flight and the ability to fly to Europe during the course of a morning, they are not talking poppycock. . . . We are standing now in the doorway of stratospheric flight. We are on the threshold of the day when New York and Paris will be no more than three or four hours apart; in other words, the Atlantic is about to shrink 75 per cent.

Since this was written in 1944, comment, I think, is unnecessary.

> World military aviation must be a world organization. The loyalties of its members must be world loyalties. It must be a strong force. To be a member of it, to wear its uniform, to hold its commission, must be the highest honour to which a young man may aspire. It will police the world. It would not waste one moment in talking before raising plain, ordinary hell with anybody in the world who committed an infraction of the rules of peace, in fact or in spirit.

Even when this first appeared I regarded it as somewhat idealistic. It seemed to ignore the realities of trying to unite different peoples, diverse theologies, religions, colours and creeds. Still, even if it was unrealistic, I suppose it probably needed to be said. I am sure that today's female military flyers and astronauts, might consider this paragraph chauvinistic.

* * *

Winged Peace paints a frightening picture of a future war even without nuclear weapons (at time of publication that still lay in the future)—of projectiles, rocket and jet-powered, raining down on cities. Having been exposed to the German V-1 flying bombs and the V-2 rockets, I can attest that this picture was no exaggeration. Atomic warheads would simply mean greater, quicker destruction.

For that reason precisely, my father approved of the Truman–Churchill decision to drop the atom bombs on Japan. It ended the war abruptly and thus saved countless lives on both sides. It also kept the Russians out. He disagreed with the argument that the second bomb need not have been dropped on Nagasaki, but could have been dropped off-shore simply to demonstrate that the U.S. had more than one in its arsenal. He felt that it would have been interpreted as showing weakness of resolve. This was total war and not a time for compassion.

By this time, William Avery Bishop had returned to civilian life as an oil company executive and was too involved with his business interests to formally concern himself with military aviation matters any longer. But he certainly did not lose interest. I have described his declining years in my biography *The Courage of the Early Morning* and do not wish to fly that same glide path again.

But vis-a-vis what he had written in *Winged Peace*, the reader is entitled to know how my father viewed certain factors concerning aviation, not just military but also general, throughout the remaining 1940's and early 1950's.

During the Korean War, the R.C.A.F.'s contribution consisted of ferrying troops, mail, and freight by North Stars from McChord Field at Tacoma, Washington, to Tokyo and Misawa in Japan, with refuelling stops at Alaska and the Aleutians en route. In all, a round-trip of 20 hours flying time. During the nearly four years that war lasted, Canadians flew 7,000,000 pounds of freight and 13,000 passengers, and chalked up 34,000 flying hours without a single loss of life or cargo.

Canada had no combat units for service in Korea, but many of our fighter pilots—22 R.C.A.F. officers—flew F-86 Sabres with the U.S. Air Force. They destroyed nine communist aircraft, probably destroyed two others, and damaged eight with the loss of only one of their own.

On that basis, I feel we have some right to our own views on how that air war was prosecuted. Privately, my father thought that the United States on behalf of the United Nations should have used the threat of nuclear power as a weapon to bring about a North Korean capitulation. This is still open to speculation. Had it actually been used, would the U.S. have lost face on moral grounds? Who can tell? Perhaps behind the scenes it was employed as a means of intimidation. We may never know. At any rate, the air war never accelerated beyond a tactical role. My father thought that at the very least it should have graduated to strategical bombing of Chinese cities north of the Korean border. This ran contrary to general policy and thinking—the exception being MacArthur. Neither Churchill nor Truman wanted to escalate the war beyond an isolated conflict. My father thought that such containment was impractical.

He was chagrined at the French bungling in Indo-China. In particular, he was annoyed that no effort was made to resist by using air power, either tactical or strategical. He went so far as to express his views in public this time, to a group of French military officials visiting Montreal.

My father certainly applauded the formation of N.A.T.O. in Europe, which was formed on August 24, 1949, and Canada's participation (along with eleven other nations) in it. By the fall of 1952, Canada had three squadrons in France, the first Canadian military services to be based on the continent since March of 1946. He did not agree with participating in S.E.A.T.O., however, although this was never seriously considered. He thought that we would have been spreading ourselves too thin by trying to participate in defending both sides of the world.

After the war, he became great friends with Gordon McGregor, who had been my airfield commander in France during World War II. Returning to civilian life, the former McKee and Webster air trophy winner, the first R.C.A.F. officer to be decorated in World War II, McGregor became president of Trans-Canada Air Lines (later Air Canada). My father was impressed with McGregor's administrative ability and thought that the airline was one of the best run in the world.

Many of my father's friends were directors of Canadair in Montreal. Here he was as pleased as I that Robert McNair, then a Group Captain in the R.C.A.F. (he had once been my Wing Commander, Flying), selected the F-86 Sabre fighter to be manufactured by that company for our N.A.T.O. squadrons. He deplored a suggestion to design our own aircraft when we could save the time and expense by building a fighter that had already been flight and combat tested. Besides, he asserted, anything we came up with by ourselves might not be, almost certainly could not be, compatible with what our allies flew. This was a carry-over from the days between the two world wars when Canada made a very feeble attempt at designing its own fighter. My father soon warmed, however, to the CF-100 fighter made by Avro in Toronto, which began rolling off the line in 1951.

During the federal election of 1950, George Drew, a close friend and the head of the Conservative party, took aim on Canadair to make political hay in Quebec. This earned him a sharp rebuke from my father, who said that if Drew didn't lay off he would leave my father with no alternative but to vote Liberal. (He did—for Brooke Claxton, the Defence Minister, with whom, ironically, he rarely agreed on air matters: the CF-100 for one.)

In those later years, he regularly attended air shows. He thought that in peacetime they were a great sales medium for the cause of aviation. I agree with that premise. On this point I must mention that for some years I was proud to serve as a director of the Canadian International Air Show, the largest—and I like to think the best—of its kind in the world.

As a final note, William Avery Bishop never lost complete touch with the service he had helped to build. He was proud of all it stood for and of how it had perpetuated. As the threat of the Cold War intensified, the R.C.A.F., which at the end of World War II had slashed its strength, now gradually began rebuilding. By 1951 it reached the 25,000 mark; a year later, it had grown to a strength of 35,000.

I do not need to ask myself what would have been my father's opinion of the standardization of uniforms under the tri-service transformation—when the air force blue disappeared for a time. I know he would have been just as angry as the rest of us, but just as overjoyed when the old colour was restored.

On July 10, 1987, my sister and I attended the dedication ceremonies at the opening of the Bishop Building, the new Canadian Forces Air Command Headquarters in Winnipeg that had been named in his honour. I know he would have been as proud as we are and just as pleased with that magnificent structure which stands in his memory.